W9-BUW-434

Miguel A. Roig-Francolí
College-Conservatory of Music
University of Cincinnati

Anthology of Post-Tonal Music

FOR USE WITH

Understanding Post-Tonal Music

McGraw Hill

Boston Burr Ridge, IL Dubuque, IA Madison, WI New York San Francisco St. Louis
Bangkok Bogotá Caracas Kuala Lumpur Lisbon London Madrid Mexico City
Milan Montreal New Delhi Santiago Seoul Singapore Sydney Taipei Toronto

The McGraw-Hill Companies

Mc Graw Hill Higher Education

Published by McGraw-Hill, an imprint of The McGraw-Hill Companies, Inc., 1221 Avenue of the Americas, New York, NY 10020. Copyright © 2008. All rights reserved. No part of this publication may be reproduced or distributed in any form or by any means, or stored in a database or retrieval system, without the prior written consent of The McGraw-Hill Companies, Inc., including, but not limited to, in any network or other electronic storage or transmission, or broadcast for distance learning.

This book is printed on acid-free paper.

10 11 12 13 14 15 QVS 20 19 18 17 16

ISBN: 978-0-07-332502-6
MHID: 0-07-332502-3

Editor in Chief: *Emily Barrosse*
Publisher: *Lisa Moore*
Sponsoring Editor: *Chris Freitag*
Editorial Assistant: *Marley Magaziner*
Marketing Manager: *Pam Cooper*
Developmental Editor: *Beth Baugh*
Associate Production Editor: *Alison Meier*
Design Manager: *Kim Menning*
Cover Designer: *Margarite Reynolds*
Production Supervisor: *Louis Swaim*
Composition: *10/12 Times by Noyes Composition and Graphics*

Cover: Cover: Vicente Pascual. *In Illo Tempore IV* and *In Illo Tempore XIX*. 2003. Mixed media on canvas. © 2007 Artists Rights Society, New York/VEGAP, Madrid.

Credits: The credits section for this book begins on page 213 and is considered an extension of the copyright page.

The Internet addresses listed in the text were accurate at the time of publication. The inclusion of a Web site does not indicate an endorsement by the authors or McGraw-Hill, and McGraw-Hill does not guarantee the accuracy of the information presented at these sites.

www.mhhe.com

Contents

Preface iv

1. Claude Debussy (1862–1918), "La cathédrale engloutie," no. 10 from *Preludes*, Book I (1910) 1
2. Claude Debussy, "Canope," no. 10 from *Preludes*, Book II (1910–13) 6
3. Claude Debussy, "Sarabande," from *Pour le piano* (1894–1901) 8
4. Igor Stravinsky (1882–1971), Introduction to Part I, from *The Rite of Spring* (1913) 12
5. Béla Bartók (1881–1945), "Song of the Harvest," no. 33 from *Forty-four Violin Duets* (1931) 23
6. Béla Bartók, "Whole-tone Scale," no. 136 from *Mikrokosmos*, vol. 5 (1932–39) 24
7. Béla Bartók, "Diminished Fifth," no. 101 from *Mikrokosmos*, vol. 4 (1932–39) 27
8. Béla Bartók, "From the Island of Bali," no. 109 from *Mikrokosmos*, vol. 4 (1932–39) 28
9. Anton Webern (1883–1945), Five Movements for String Quartet, op. 5, II (1909) 30
10. Anton Webern, Five Movements for String Quartet, op. 5, III (1909) 31
11. Arnold Schoenberg (1874–1951), "Angst und Hoffen," no. 7 from *Book of the Hanging Gardens*, op. 15 (1909) 33
12. Alban Berg (1885–1935), "Schlafend trägt man mich," no. 2 from *Four Songs*, op. 2 (1908–1909) 36
13. Igor Stravinsky (1882–1971), *Agnus Dei*, from Mass (1944–48) 38
14. Paul Hindemith (1895–1963), Interlude in G, from *Ludus tonalis* (1942) 42
15. Paul Hindemith, "Vom Tode Mariä I," from *Das Marienleben* (1923) 43
16. Charles Ives (1874–1954), "The Things Our Fathers Loved," from *114 Songs* (ca. 1917) 50
17. Charles Ives, "The Cage," from *114 Songs* (1906) 52
18. Ruth Crawford Seeger (1901–1953), *Diaphonic Suite* no. 4, III (1930) 53
19. Luigi Dallapiccola (1904–1975), "Contrapunctus secundus," no. 5 from *Quaderno musicale di Annalibera* (1952–53) 57
20. Luigi Dallapiccola, "Quartina," no. 11 from *Quaderno musicale di Annalibera* (1952–53) 58
21. Anton Webern (1883–1945), "Wie bin ich froh," no. 1 from *Drei Lieder*, op. 25 (1935) 59
22. Anton Webern, Piano Variations, op. 27, II (1935–36) 61
23. Arnold Schoenberg (1874–1951), *Klavierstück*, op. 33a (1929) 62
24. Igor Stravinsky (1882–1971), "Lacrimosa," from *Requiem Canticles* (1966) 67
25. Pierre Boulez (b. 1925), *Structures Ia*, mm. 1–39 (1952) 72
26. Milton Babbitt (b. 1916), *Composition for Twelve Instruments*, mm. 1–26 (1948) 78
27. Olivier Messiaen (1908–1992), *Turangalîla Symphony*, Introduction, reh. 12–22 (1946–48) 84
28. Elliott Carter (b. 1908), String Quartet no. 2, I, mm. 35–134 (1959) 103
29. Karlheinz Stockhausen (b. 1928), *Stimmung* (three pages: *Formschema*, one sample page of *Modelle*, and one sample page of *Magische Namen*) (1968) 108
30. John Cage (1912–1992), *Winter Music* (one page) (1957) 111
31. Witold Lutosławski (1913–1994), *Jeux vénitiens*, I (1960–61) 112
32. György Ligeti (1923–2006), *Ramifications*, mm. 1–44 (1968–69) 116
33. George Rochberg (1918–2005), *Music for the Magic Theater*, reh. 1–17 (1965) 140
34. Luciano Berio (1925–2003), *Sinfonia*, III ("In ruhig fliessender Bewegung"), mm. 1–120 (to reh. F) (1968) 158
35. George Crumb (b. 1923), "Dream Images (Love–Death Music)," no. 11 from *Makrokosmos*, vol. 1 (1972–73) 172
36. Steve Reich (b. 1936), *Violin Phase* (1967) 174
37. Louis Andriessen (b. 1939), *De Staat*, mm. 1–161 (1972–76) 182
38. Arvo Pärt (b. 1935), *Cantus* (1977) 194
39. Augusta Read Thomas (b. 1964), *Spring Song*, mm. 1–41 (1995) 199
40. Thomas Adès (b. 1971), *Asyla*, II, mm. 1–43 (1997) 201
41. Kaija Saariaho (b. 1952), *Ariel's Hail* (2000) 207

Acknowledgment of Sources 213

Preface

This anthology is meant to be used in conjunction with the study of the textbook *Understanding Post-Tonal Music*. The book includes detailed analyses of a total of thirty-two pieces by twenty-five composers, ranging chronologically from Claude Debussy and Igor Stravinsky to Kaija Saariaho, Augusta Read Thomas, and Thomas Adès. All these thirty-two pieces are included in the anthology. Whenever possible, complete pieces or movements have been used. If a composition or movement is particularly long, a substantial and representative fragment has been chosen for analysis and inclusion in the anthology. The remaining nine compositions in the anthology are used for analytical assignments in the textbook. The total number of pieces in the anthology is thus forty-one, by twenty-six composers. Because of the close relationship between the book and the anthology, the latter is not meant to be an optional supplement to the book, but rather an essential and required component of the pedagogical packet.

The exact correspondence between book chapters and anthology pieces is as follows:

Chapter 1. Pitch Centricity and Composition with Motivic Cells

Analysis 1.1. Debussy, "La cathédrale engloutie," from *Preludes*, Book I (Anthology no. 1)

Analysis 1.2. Stravinsky, Introduction to Part I, from *The Rite of Spring* (Anthology no. 4)

Anthology nos. 2 and 3 are used for assignments.

Chapter 2. Pitch Centricity and Symmetry

Analysis 2.1. Bartók, "Song of the Harvest," from *Forty-four Violin Duets* (Anthology no. 5)

Analysis 2.2. Bartók, "Whole-tone Scale," from *Mikrokosmos*, vol. 5 (Anthology no. 6)

Anthology nos. 7 and 8 are used for assignments.

Chapter 3. Introduction to Pitch-Class-Set Theory

No pieces from the anthology are used in this chapter.

Chapter 4. Analyzing Atonal Music

Analysis 4.1. Webern, "Five Movements for String Quartet," op. 5, III (Anthology no. 10)

Analysis 4.2. Schoenberg "Angst und Hoffen," no. 7 from *Book of the Hanging Gardens*, op. 15 (Anthology no. 11)

Anthology nos. 9 and 12 are used for assignments.

Chapter 5. Drawing on (and Reinterpreting) the Past . . .

Analysis 5.1. Stravinsky, *Agnus Dei*, from Mass (Anthology no. 13)

Analysis 5.2. Hindemith, Interlude in G, from *Ludus tonalis* (Anthology no. 14)

Anthology no. 15 is used for an assignment.

Chapter 6. . . . And Inventing the Future

Ives and Musical Borrowing (includes a discussion of Anthology no. 16, Charles Ives's "The Things Our Fathers Loved," from *114 Songs*)

Analysis 6.1. Ives, "The Cage" (Anthology no. 17)

Analysis 6.2. Crawford, *Diaphonic Suite* no. 4, III (Anthology no. 18)

Chapter 7. Twelve-Tone Music I: An Introduction

Analysis 7.1. Dallapiccola, "Contrapunctus secundus," from *Quaderno musicale di Annalibera* (Anthology no. 19)

Analysis 7.2. Dallapiccola, "Quartina," from *Quaderno musicale di Annalibera* (Anthology no. 20)
Anthology no. 21 is used for an assignment.

Chapter 8. Twelve-Tone Music II: Invariance, Symmetry, and Combinatoriality

Analysis 8.1. Webern, Piano Variations, op. 27, II (Anthology no. 22)

Analysis 8.2. Schoenberg, *Klavierstück*, op. 33a (Anthology no. 23)

Chapter 9. Serialism: Developments After 1945

Analysis 9.1. Stravinsky, "Lacrimosa," from *Requiem Canticles* (Anthology no. 24)

Analysis 9.2. Boulez, *Structures Ia* (Anthology no. 25)

Analysis 9.3. Babbitt, *Composition for Twelve Instruments* (Anthology no. 26)

Chapter 10. Expanding the Limits of Musical Temporality

Analysis 10.1. Messiaen, Introduction, from *Turangalîla Symphony* (Anthology, no. 27)

Analysis 10.2. Musical Characters in the Second String Quartet, I (Anthology no. 28)

Analysis 10.3. Stockhausen, *Stimmung* (Anthology no. 29)

Chapter 11. Aleatory Music, Sound Mass, and Beyond

Analysis 11.1. Cage, *Winter Music* (Anthology no. 30)

Analysis 11.2. Lutosławki, *Jeux vénitiens*, I (Anthology no. 31)

Analysis 11.3. Ligeti, *Ramifications*, mm. 1–38 (Anthology no. 32)

Chapter 12. Where Past and Future Meet . . .

Analysis 12.1. Rochberg, *Music for the Magic Theater*, reh. 1–17 (Anthology no. 33)

Analysis 12.2. Berio, *Sinfonia*, III (Anthology no. 34)

Anthology no. 35 is used for an assignment.

Chapter 13. Simplifying Means

Analysis 13.1. Reich, *Violin Phase* (Anthology no. 36)

Analysis 13.2. Andriessen, *De Staat*, mm. 1–161 (Anthology no. 37)

Analysis 13.3. Pärt, *Cantus* (Anthology no. 38)

Chapter 14. Into the Twenty-First Century

Analysis 14.1. Thomas, *Spring Song* (Anthology no. 39)

Analysis 14.2. Adès, *Asyla*, II (Anthology no. 40)

Analysis 14.3. Saariaho, *Ariel's Hail* (Anthology no. 41)

The organization of the anthology thus follows the organization of the textbook, which is designed according to a roughly chronological plan and, within that, by general topics. This modular organization following two simultaneous criteria acknowledges that twentieth-century music is best understood not only in technical terms, but also in a historical context, and that stylistic and compositional developments do not take place in a historical vacuum.

An initial general topic, pitch centricity, covers music by Debussy, early Stravinsky, and Bartók in Chapters 1 and 2. The next topic, atonal music, is covered in Chapters 3 and 4. In Chapter 3, pitch-class sets are studied formally, setting the stage for the analyses of Webern and Schoenberg atonal pieces in Chapter 4. Chapters 5 and 6 discuss two seemingly contradictory, yet highly complementary, stylistic trends: neoclassicism, as found in the music of Stravinsky and Hindemith, and ultramodernism, as found in Ives and Crawford. Chapters 7 and 8 are devoted to the study of "classical" twelve-tone music, with reference to works by Dallapiccola, Schoenberg, Berg, and Webern, and Chapter 9 deals with serial practices after World War II, as illustrated by Stravinsky, Boulez, and Babbitt.

Chapter 9 thus provides a link between music before and after World War II. Post–World War II music is covered in the last six chapters (9 through 14). The general topics in these chapters, and following serialism, are issues of temporality (Chapter 10, including analyses of music by Messiaen, Carter, and Stockhausen), aleatory composition, sound mass, and other post-serial techniques (Chapter 11, with reference to Cage, Lutosławski, and Ligeti), quotation and collage (Chapter 12, with focus on Rochberg and Berio), minimalism (Chapter 13, which includes analyses of music by Reich, Andriessen, and Pärt), and finally a review of some of the most recent compositional trends as found in pieces by Thomas, Adès, and Saariaho (Chapter 14).

Miguel A. Roig-Francolí
College-Conservatory of Music
University of Cincinnati

1. Claude Debussy (1862-1918)

"La cathédrale engloutie," no. 10 from *Preludes*, Book I (1910)

B pentatonic
⟨Peu à peu sortant de la brume⟩
sempre pp
(pp)
p marqué
p
Augmentez progressivement ⟨Sans presser⟩
pentatonic
(F)GACD
8a
f
più f
V
acting
end of A
Sonore sans dureté
planning
ff
8a bassa
6/4 chords
C pp

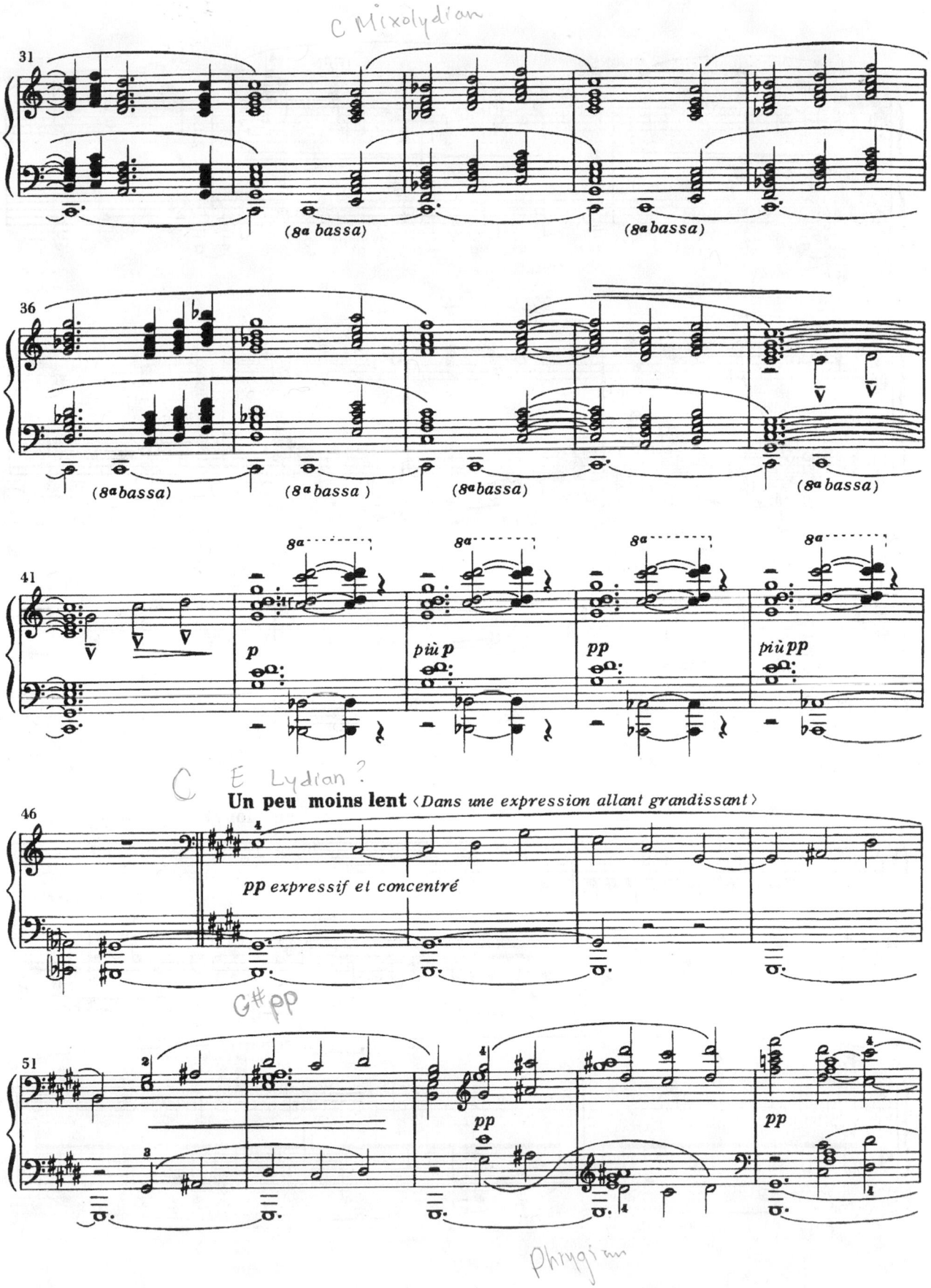
C Mixolydian
31
(8a bassa)
(8a bassa)
36
(8a bassa)
(8a bassa)
(8a bassa)
(8a bassa)
41
8a
p
più p
pp
più pp
C E Lydian?
Un peu moins lent ‹Dans une expression allant grandissant›
46
pp expressif et concentré
G# pp
51
pp
pp
Phrygian

56
p
f
8a
60
8a
molto
dim.
chromatic planing
64
p
p
70
pp
au Mouv.t
C Mixolyd.
pp
Comme un écho de la phrase entendue précédemment
8a bassa
(Flottant et sourd)
pentatonic ostinato
73
8a bassa

feels like center even tho C
76
8a bassa
79
8a bassa
82
più pp
Dans la sonorité du début
pp
8a bassa
85
8a
8a
8a

2. Claude Debussy

"Canope," no. 10 from *Preludes*, Book II (1910-13)

18
? mi b
p marqué
pp
22
p marqué
p
pp
1er Mouvement
25
p
pp
pp
p
29
retenu - // Plus lent
très doux et très expressif
Très lent
encore plus doux
più p
pp
più pp

3. Claude Debussy

"Sarabande," from *Pour le piano* (1894-1901)

retenu (restrained)
au mouvt (first tempo)
plus p(softer)
pp
p
u.c.
mf
dim.
mysterieux (mysteriously)

animez un peu (gradually faster)
très soutenu (very sustained)
33
mp
p
38
p
au mouvt (first tempo)
42
f
f
46
p
p
plus p (softer)
u.c.

51
mf
cresc.
f
56
ff
triste (sadly)
p
61
più p
5 4 3 4
66
p dim.
u.c.
retenu (restrained)
plus p (softer)
pp
ppp
m.d.
r.h.

4. Igor Stravinsky (1882-1971)

Introduction to Part I, from *The Rite of Spring* (1913)

2
solo
p espress.
3
in tempo
Più mosso
C. ingl.
Cl. (A)
Cl. b. (B)
poco più f
Fag.
4
Ob.
C. ingl.
Cl. picc. (D)
solo
espress.
Cl. (A)
Fag.
Cor.
II.III.IV
V-ni II
pizz.
V-le

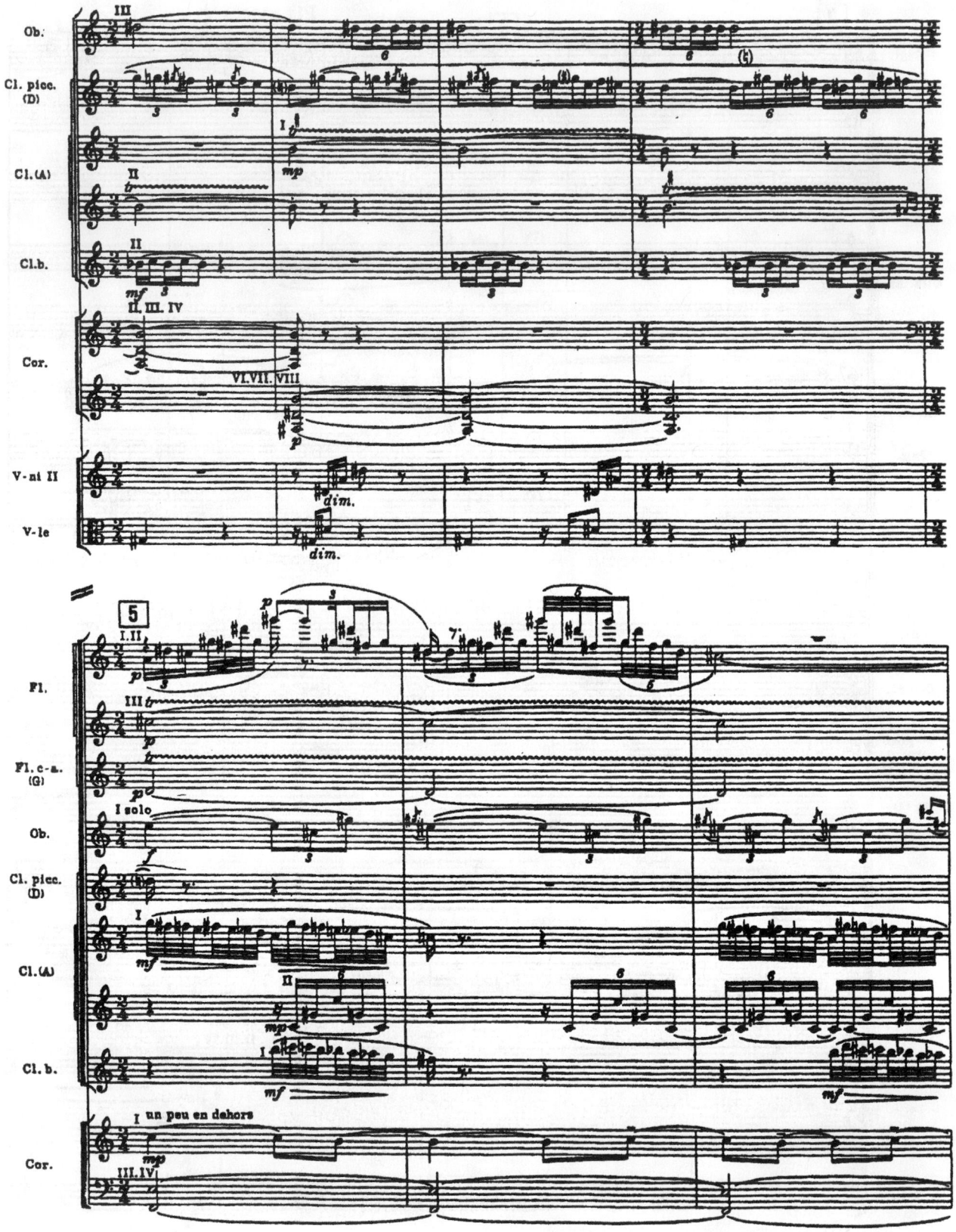
Ob.
Cl. picc. (D)
Cl. (A)
Cl. b.
Cor.
V-ni II
V-le
dim.
dim.
5
Fl.
Fl. c-a. (G)
Ob.
I solo
Cl. picc. (D)
Cl. (A)
Cl. b.
Cor.
un peu en dehors

6
Fl.
Fl. c-a. (G)
solo
Ob.
I
C. ingl.
solo (en dehors)
Cl. (A)
II
Cl.b.
solo
Fag.
Cor.
III. IV
Fl.
Fl. III = Picc. II
Fl. c-a. (G)
C. ingl.
V-ně I

7
Picc.
Fl.
Fl. c-a. (G)
Ob.
C. ingl.
Cl. picc. (D)
Cl. (A)
Cl. b.
Fag.
Cor.
V-c. solo
trem.
solo
legato
mf espress.
pizz.
I solo
(très en dehors)
8
Fl.
Fl. c-a. (G)
C. ingl.
Cl. picc. (D)
Cl. (A)
Cl. b.
Fag.
C-fag.
Cor.
C-b. solo
dim.
poco più
Cl. b. II = Cl. III (B)

9
Fl.
Fl. c-a. (G)
Ob.
I solo
Cl. picc. (D)
Cl. (A)
Cl. II in A=Cl. II in B
Fag.
C-fag.
C-b. solo
Fl.
Fl. c-a. (G)
Ob.
Cl. picc. (D)
solo
Cl. (B)

10
Fl.
Fl. c-a. (G)
Ob.
C. ingl.
solo
Cl. picc. (D)
solo
sempre ff
(A)
Cl.
très en dehors
(B)
C-fag.
mf
mf
V-c. solo
II con sord. (arco)
6 C-b.
con sord.
pizz.

Picc.
Fl.
I Flatterzunge
II
Ob.
solo (come sopra)
mf
II. III Flatterzunge
C. ingl.
Cl. picc. (D)
Cl. (A)
I
III Flatterzunge
(B)
C-fag.
Tr-ba. picc. (D)
con sord.
mf
V-c. solo
6 C-b.

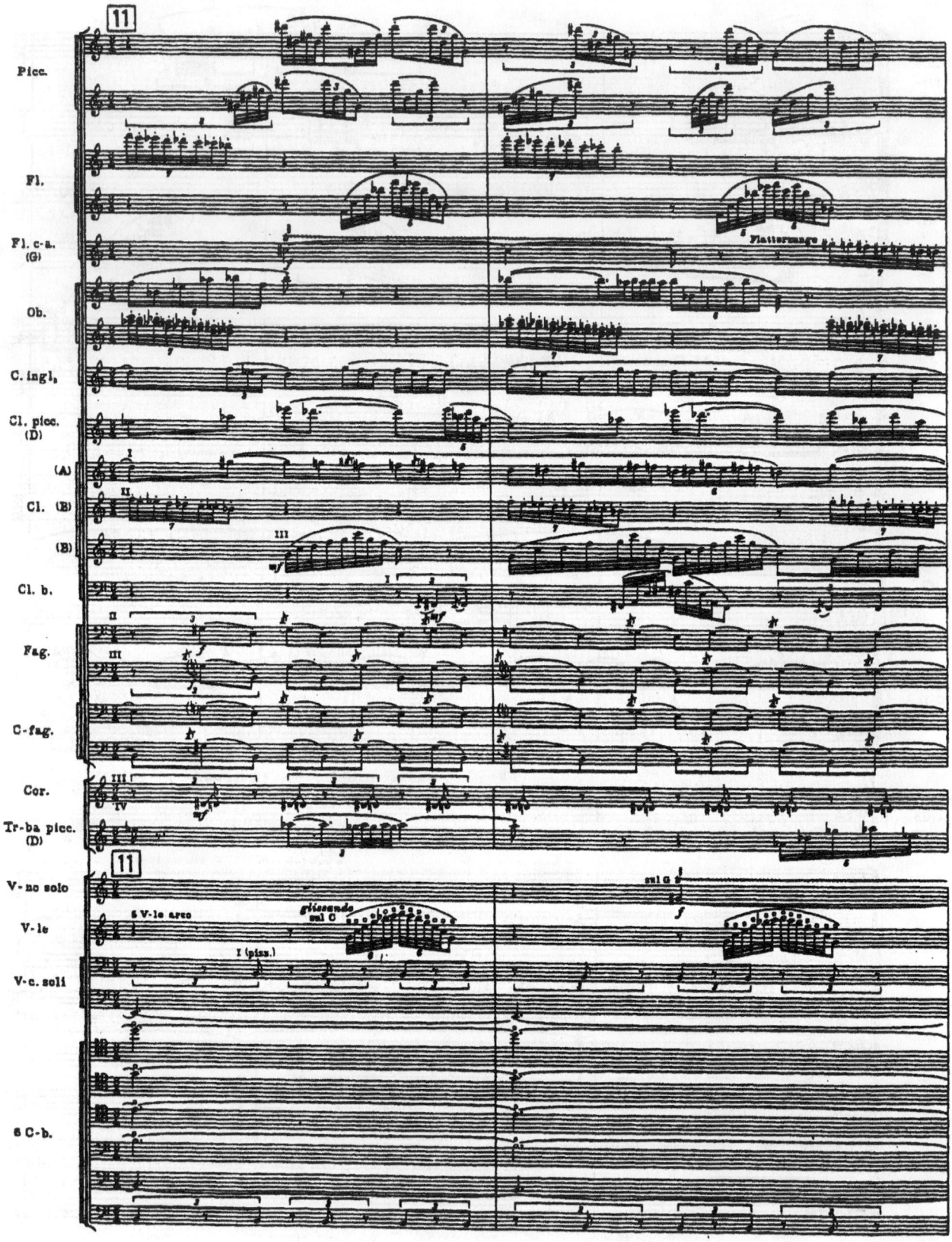
11
Picc.
Fl.
Fl. c-a. (G)
Flatterzunge
Ob.
C. ingl.
Cl. picc. (D)
(A)
Cl. (B)
(B)
Cl. b.
Fag.
C-fag.
Cor.
Tr-ba picc. (D)
11
V-no solo
sul G
V-le
5 V-le arco
glissando sul C
I (pizz.)
V-c. soli
6 C-b.

Picc.
Fl.
Fl. c-a. (G)
Ob.
C. ingl.
Cl. picc. (A)
Cl (E)
(B)
Cl. b.
II
Fag.
III
C-fag.
III.IV
Cor.
Tr-ba picc. (D)
V-no solo
V-le div.
V-c. soli
8 C-b.

12
Tempo I
Cl. (B)
solo
Fag.
(come sopra)
C-fag.
C-fag. II muta in Fag. IV
V-ni I
tutti pizz.
C-b.
Cl. picc. (D)
Cl. (A)
(B)
Cl. b.
Fag.
Cor.
I.II con sord.
V-ni I
6 V-le sole
II.III
IV.V.VI
C-b.

5. Béla Bartók (1881-1945)

"Song of the Harvest," no. 33 from *Forty-four Violin Duets* (1931)

6. Béla Bartók

"Whole-tone Scale," no. 136 from *Mikrokosmos*, vol. 5 (1932-39)

26
sotto
mf
sopra
32
p
38
Più mosso, ♩ = 138
risoluto, marcato
44
sotto
cresc.
sopra
sempre legato

palendrome

A	B	A
0 0	1 1	1 0 0
0 1	1 0	1 1 0

X

7. **Béla Bartók**

"Diminished Fifth," no. 101 from *Mikrokosmos*, vol. 4 (1932-39)

8. Béla Bartók

"From the Island of Bali," no. 109 from *Mikrokosmos*, vol. 4 (1932-39)

18
22
ff
26
poco allarg.
sf
(prol. Ped.)
31
Andante
p, dolce
m.s.
dim.
36
poco rit.
a tempo
pp
[1 min. 56 sec.]
(prol. Ped.)

9. Anton Webern (1883-1945)

Five Movements for String Quartet, op. 5, II (1909)

10. Anton Webern

Five Movements for String Quartet, op. 5, III (1909)

15
tempo (𝅗𝅥 = 84)
poco a
pizz.
pp
p
mp
mf
arco
poco cresc.
poco accel.
20
f
cresc.
mp cresc.
mf
f cresc.
sehr rasch (𝅗𝅥 = 102)
ff
fff
sfff

11. Arnold Schoenberg (1874-1951)

"Angst und Hoffen," no. 7 from *Book of the Hanging Gardens*, op. 15 (1909)

9
daß mein La - ger Trä - - - - - nen schwem - men, daß ich je - de
p
fp
f
12
Sehr langsam
(♩ = ♩)
Freu - de von mir weh - - - re, daß ich kei - nes Freundes
p
15
Trost be - geh - re.
pp

Translation of Text

"Anguish and Hope," by Stefan George

Anguish and hope in turn seize me.
My words trail off in sighing.
Such tempestuous longing assails me
That I do not turn to rest or sleep
That tears flood my couch,
That I ward off every pleasure,
That I seek no friend's consolation.

12. Alban Berg (1885-1935)

"Schlafend trägt man mich," no. 2 from *Four Songs*, op. 2 (1908-1909)

Translation of Text

"In Sleep I am Borne," by Alfred Mombert

In sleep I am borne unto my homeland.
From afar I come, over peaks, over abysses
Over a darkened sea unto my homeland.

13. Igor Stravinsky (1882-1971)
Agnus Dei, from Mass (1944-48)

15
D.
A.
T.
B.
Ob.I.II
C.I.
Fag.I.II
Tr.I.II in Do
I
Trb.
II.III
A — gnus De-i,
A — gnus De — i, qui tol-lis
23
qui tol-lis pec — ca — ta mun — di:.... mi — se — re — re no — bis.
pec — ca — ta..... mun — di:.... mi — se — re — re no — bis.

30
D.
A-gnus De-i, qui tol-lis pec-ca-ta...
A.
T.
A-gnus De-i, qui tol-lis pec-ca-ta...
B.
Ob.I.II
C.I.
Fag.I.II
Tr.I.II in Do
I
Trb.
II.III
37
D.
..... mun——di: do—na no—bis pa-cem.
A.
T.
..... mun——di: do—na no—bis pa-cem.
B.
I
Ob.
II
pp
C.I.
pp
Fag.I.II
pp
Tr.I.II in Do
pp
I
Trb.
pp
II.III
pp

Translation of Text

Lamb of God,
Who takes away the sins of the world,
Have mercy upon us.

Lamb of God,
Who takes away the sins of the world,
Have mercy upon us.

Lamb of God,
Who takes away the sins of the world,
Give us peace.

14. Paul Hindemith (1895-1963)

Interlude in G, from *Ludus tonalis* (1942)

15. Paul Hindemith

"Vom Tode Mariä I," from *Das Marienleben* (1923)

10
p
mp
ſprach: Jetzt wird es Zeit, daß du er-ſcheinſt. Und ſie er-ſchrak wie da-mals und er-wies ſich
p
pp ſehr zart
15
mf
p
wie-der als die Magd, ihn tief be-ja-hend. Er a-ber
mf
ſtrahl-te, und un-end-lich na-hend, ſchwand er wie in ihr An-ge-
p
20
ſicht, und hieß die weit-hin aus-ge-gan-ge-nen Be-keh-rer zu-

mf
25
p
Noch lang
ſam - - men-kom-men in das Haus am Hang, das Haus des A - - bendmahls.
ritenuto
mf
p
pp
ſamer (♩=104-112)
pp ſehr ruhig
Sie ka-men ſchwe-rer und tra - ten ban-ge ein: Da lag, ent-
l.H.
30
p
pp
lang die ſchma-le Bett - ſtatt, die in Un - - ter - gang und Aus-er - wäh -
mp
ruhig
35
p
- - - lung rät-ſel-haft Ge-tauch - te, ganz un - - - ver-ſehrt, wie ei-ne Un-ge-brauch-

pp
te, und ach - te - te auf eng - li - schen Ge -
pp
40
sang. Nun da sie al - le hin - ter ih - ren Ker - zen
p
ppp
pp
ab - war - ten sah, riß sie vom Ü - ber - maß der Stim - men
p
45
sich und schenk - te noch von Her - zen die bei - den Klei - der fort, die sie be - saß,
f
mp
poco f

50
nif
p
und hob ihr Antlitz auf zu dem und dem.... (O Urſprung na - men-lo-ſer Trä - - -
nif
mp
pp
55
- - - - - - nen - bä - che.)
mp
pp
ritenuto
Wie zuerſt
pp
60
Sie a - ber leg - te ſich in ih - re Schwä - - che und zog die
pp
mp
p
Him - - mel an Je ru - - - ſa - lem ſo nah her - an, daß ih - re
nif

65
See - - - le nur, aus-tre - tend, sich ein we-nig strecken muß - - te, schon hob
mf
p
70
er sie, der al - - - - - - les von ihr wuß - te,
poco f
poco f
hin - - ein in ih - re gött - - - - - -
mf
75
- - li - - che Na - tur.
p
molto riten.
p
mf
pp

Translation of Text

"On the Death of Mary," by Rainer Maria Rilke

The same great angel which had earlier brought her tidings of her conception, stood there, waiting until she noticed him. And he spoke, "It is now time that you appear." And she was frightened as before and, humbly acquiescing, became again as the maiden. Then he became radiant and, nearing her infinitely, vanished as into her face. And he called together the widely dispersed Disciples to the house on the slope, the house of the Last Supper. They came gravely and entered fearfully. There she lay, along the narrow bedstead, mysteriously immersed in her end and in her chosen state—entirely unharmed, as one unused, listening to the song of angels. Now when she saw them waiting behind their candles, she tore herself from the abundance of voices and, with a full heart, gave away the two robes which she owned. And she raised up her countenance to this one and that one. . . (O source of nameless streams of tears.) Then she sank back in weakness and drew the heavens so near to Jerusalem that her soul, setting forth, had only to stretch itself a little, for He who knew everything about her was even then raising her to her godly nature.

16. Charles Ives (1874-1954)

"The Things Our Fathers Loved," from *114 Songs* (ca. 1917)

14
all Red, White and Blue
Now! Hear the
più accel.
ff
l.h.
16
songs! I know not what are the
l.h.
18
words But they sing in my
poco rall.
r.h.
l.h.
rit.
20
soul of the things our Fath-ers loved.
p much slower
very slowly and sustained
pp
rit.
ppp

17. Charles Ives

"The Cage," from *114 Songs* (1906)

NOTE:- All notes not marked with sharp or flat are natural.

18. Ruth Crawford Seeger (1901-1953)

Diaphonic Suite no. 4, III (1930)

20
p
mp
mf
25
f
gliss.
sfz
30
mp poco più legato
p
35

40
p
mp
mf
45
f
gliss
50
presto possibile
mp
p martellato
55

60
cresc. to meas. 67
cresc. to meas. 67
65
sfz
p
70

19. Luigi Dallapiccola (1904-1975)

"Contrapunctus secundus," no. 5 from *Quaderno musicale di Annalibera* (1952-53)

20. Luigi Dallapiccola

"Quartina," no. 11 from *Quaderno musicale di Annalibera* (1952-53)

21. Anton Webern (1883-1945)

"Wie bin ich froh," no. 1 from *Drei Lieder*, op. 25 (1935)

7
8
rit. - - - - - tempo
blühn_ die Blu - men mir die Welt! noch ein -
world_ is o - ver - grown with flow'rs! Once more
9
10
rit. - - - - -
mal_ bin ich ganz ins Wer - den hin - ge - stellt
I_ in cre - a - - tion's por - tal live my hours,
sehr langsam ♩ = ca 42
11
12
tempo I
und bin auf Er - den.
and yet am mor - tal.

ca 1'

① axis of symmetry – E♭ – A (double)

② articulation
- slurred
- legato
- scat.
- viennese

(816)

22. Anton Webern

Piano Variations, op. 27, II (1935-36)

23. Arnold Schoenberg (1874-1951)

Klavierstück, op. 33a (1929)

P10 **Mäßig** ♩= 120

cantabile

p

sfp

fp

sfp

nf

p

poco rit

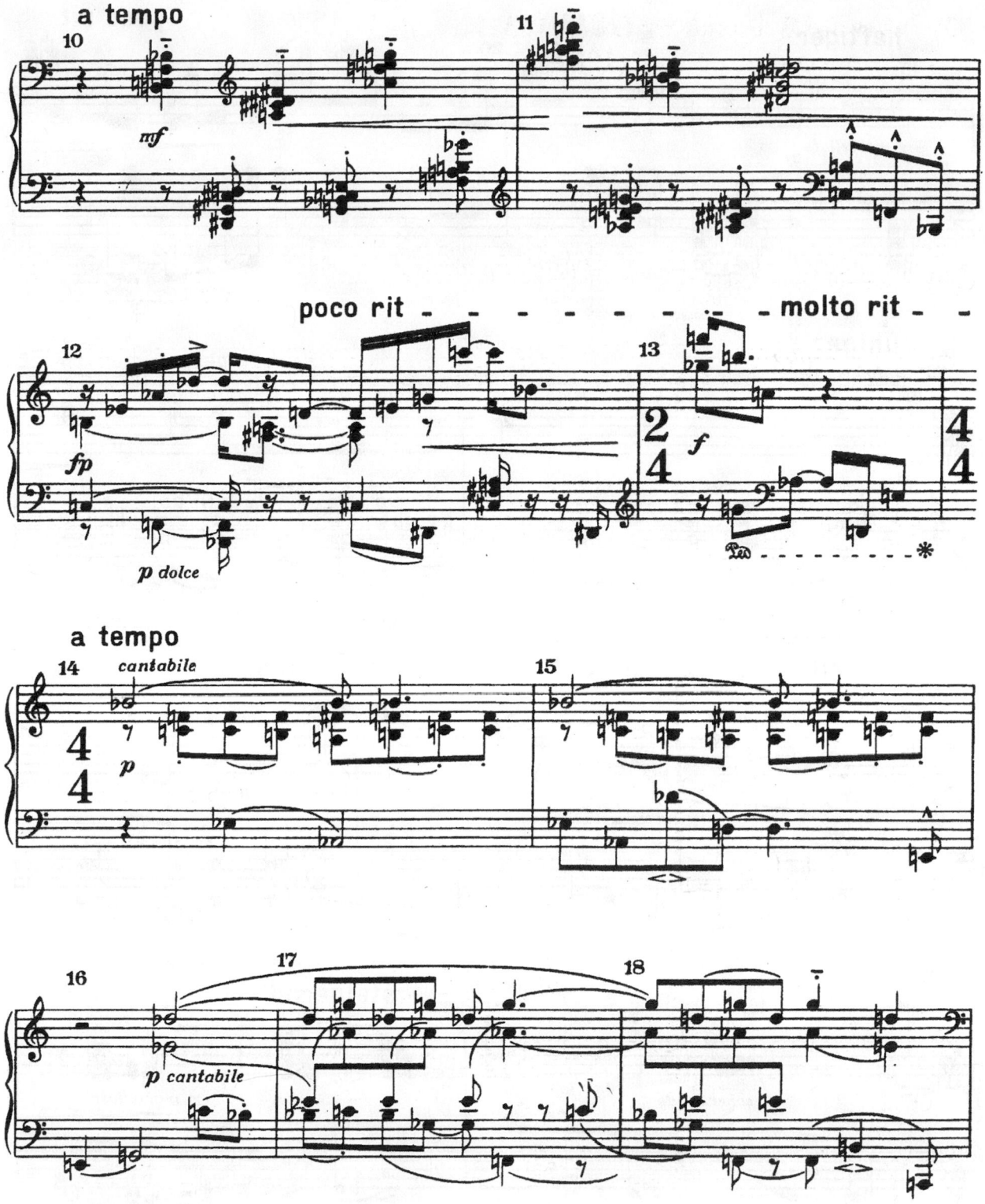
a tempo
10
11
mf
poco rit
molto rit
12
13
fp
p dolce
f
a tempo
14
15
cantabile
p
16
17
18
p cantabile

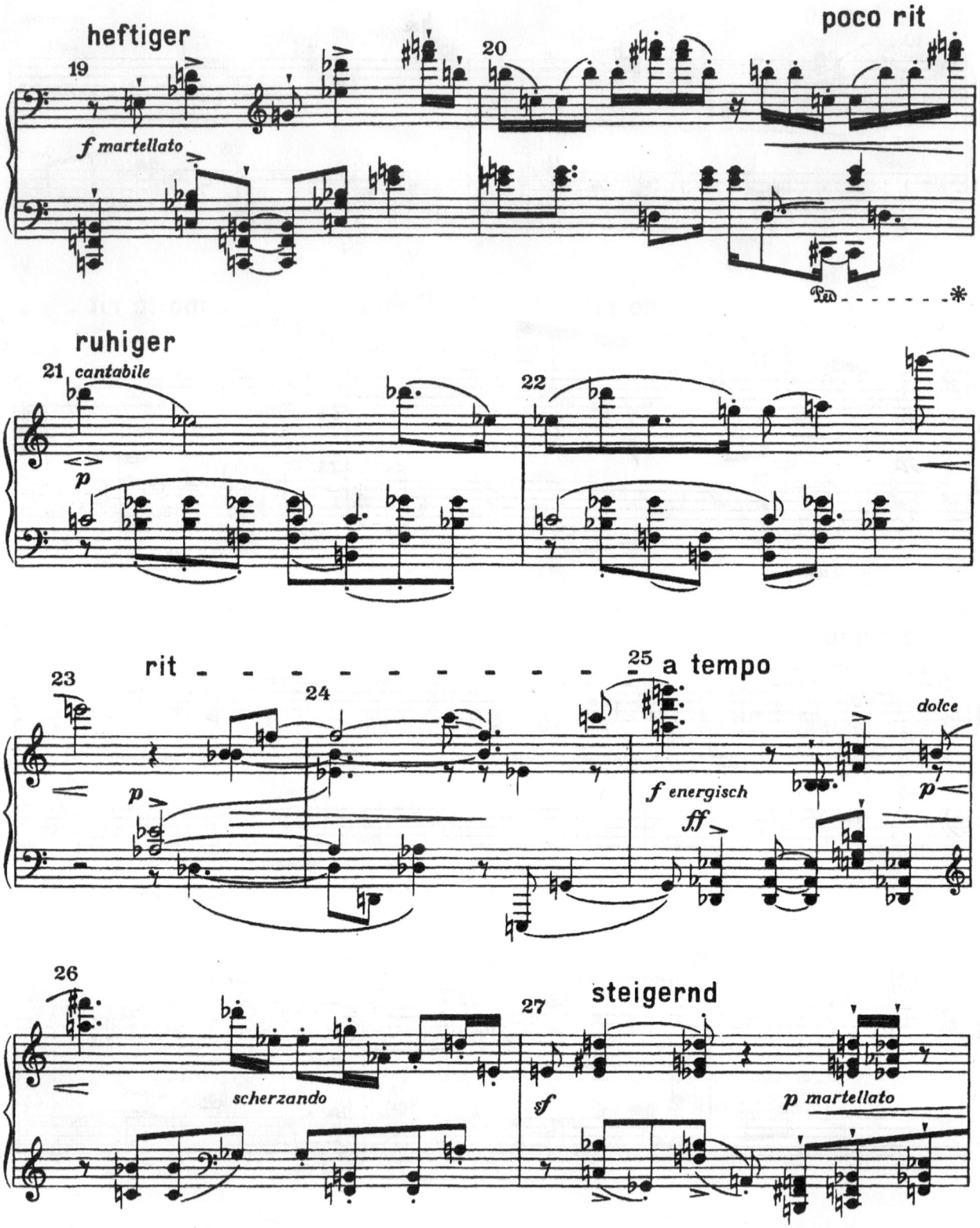
heftiger
19
f martellato
20
poco rit
ruhiger
21
cantabile
p
22
23
rit
24
25
a tempo
dolce
f energisch
ff
p
26
scherzando
27
steigernd
f
p martellato

28
f
f
29
8
30
f
31
mp
5
4

32
33
ff
p
rit - - - - Ruhig
34
35
p dolce
36
37
steigernd
p cresc.
38
39
rit - - - - - - - -
40
f
ff

24. Igor Stravinsky (1882-1971)
"Lacrimosa," from *Requiem Canticles* (1966)

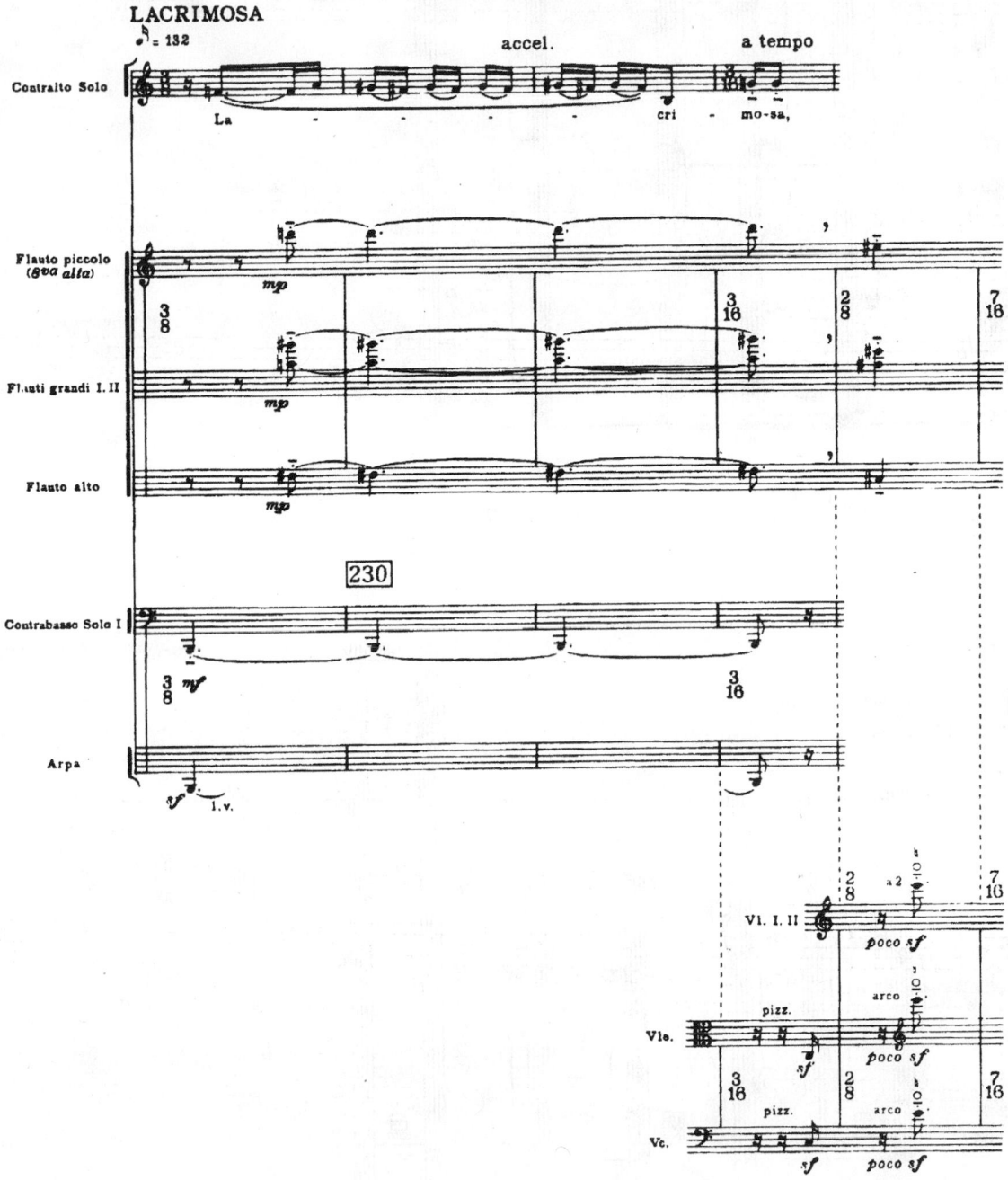

N.B.: All instruments in this score are notated in C.

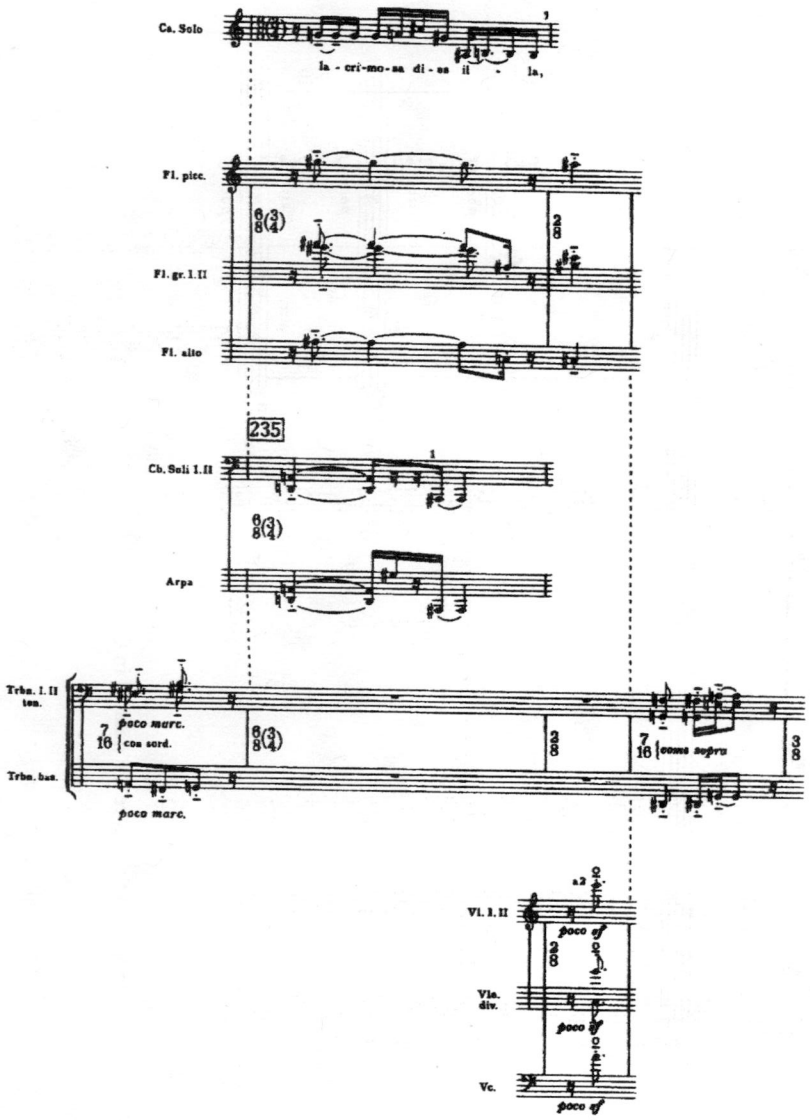
Ca. Solo
la - cri-mo-sa di - es il - la,
Fl. picc.
Fl. gr. I. II
Fl. alto
235
Cb. Soli I. II
Arpa
Trbn. I. II ten.
poco marc.
con sord.
come sopra
Trbn. bas.
poco marc.
Vl. I. II
a2
poco sf
Vla. div.
poco sf
Vc.
poco sf

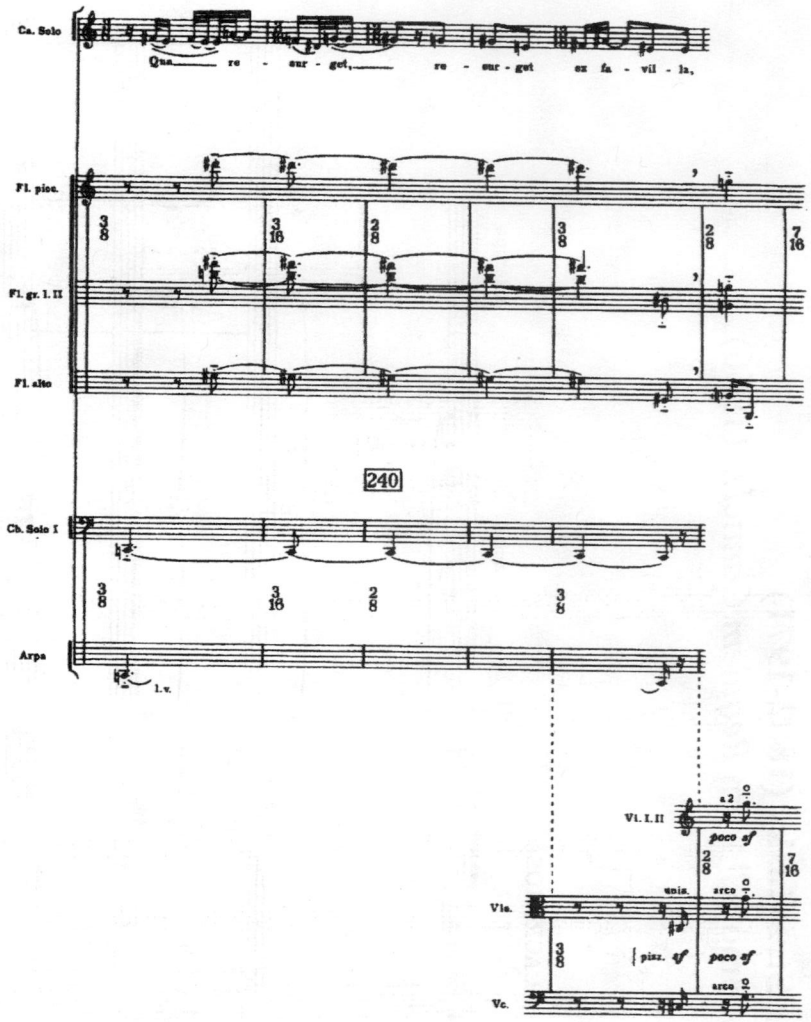
Ca. Solo
Qua re - sur - get, re - sur - get ex fa - vil - la,
Fl. picc.
Fl. gr. I. II
Fl. alto
240
Ch. Solo I
Arpa
l. v.
Vl. I. II
a2
poco sf
Vla.
unis.
arco
pizz. sf
poco sf
Vc.
arco

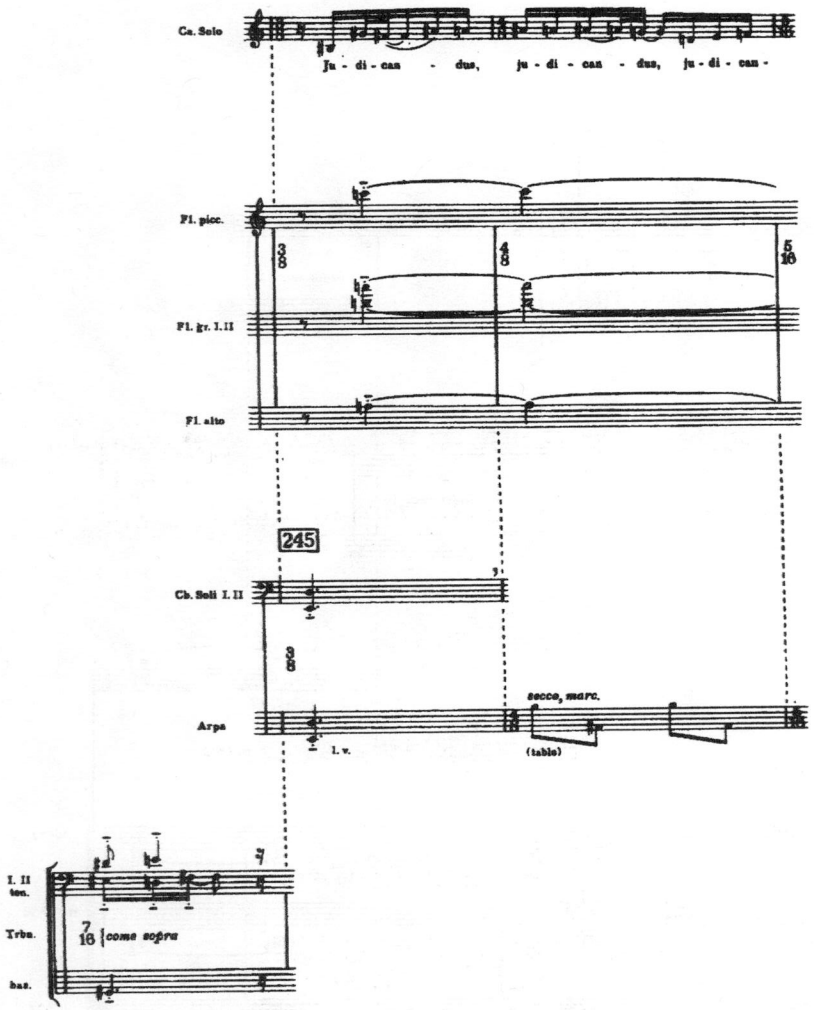
Ca. Solo
Ju - di - can - dus, ju - di - can - dus, ju - di - can -
Fl. picc.
Fl. gr. I. II
Fl. alto
245
Cb. Soli I. II
Arpa
secco, marc.
(table)
I. v.
I. II ten.
Trbn.
bas.
come sopra

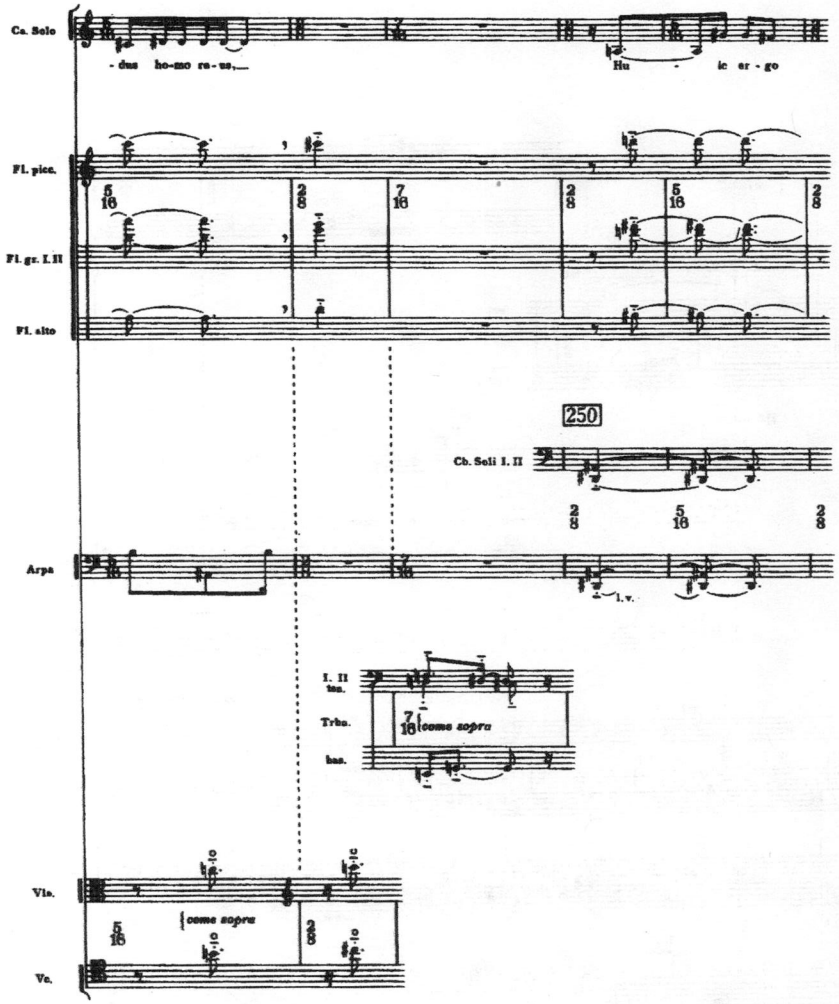
Ca. Solo
- dus ho-mo re-us,
Hu - ic er - go
Fl. picc.
Fl. gr. I. II
Fl. alto
250
Cb. Soli I. II
Arpa
I. v.
I. II ten.
Trbn.
bas.
come sopra
Vln.
Vc.

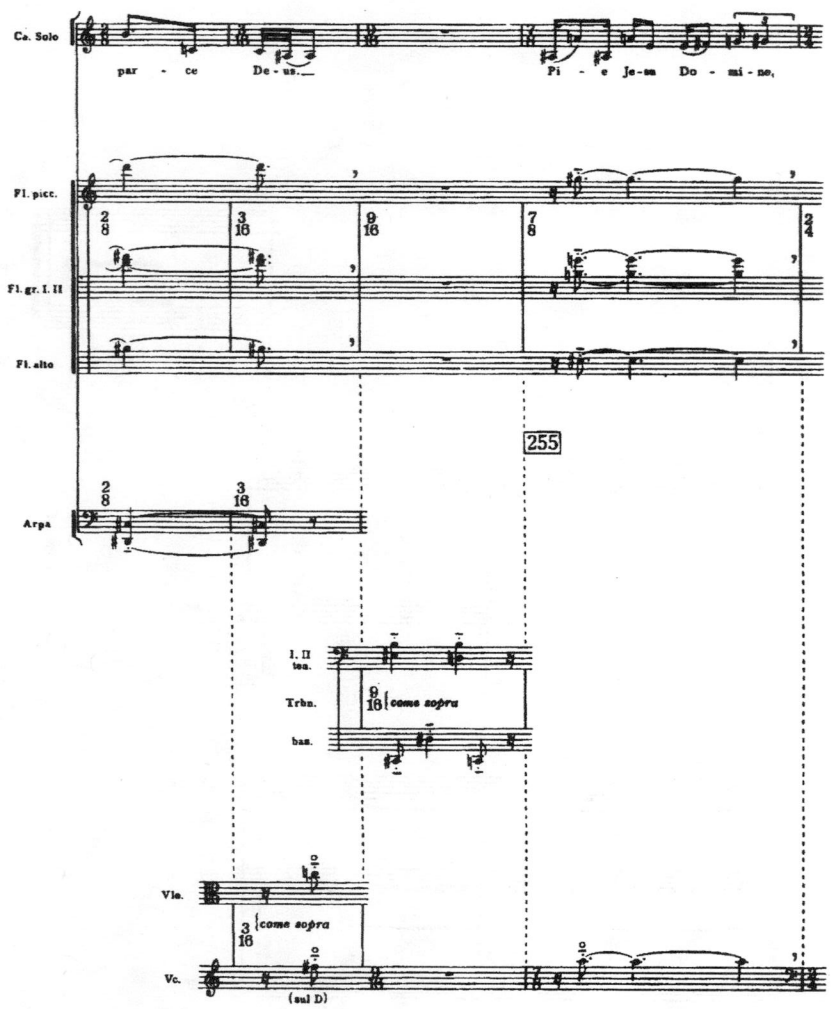
Ca. Solo
par - ce De - us.
Pi - e Je-su Do - mi - ne,
Fl. picc.
Fl. gr. I. II
Fl. alto
255
Arpa
I. II ten.
Trbn.
bas.
come sopra
Vla.
Vc.
(sul D)

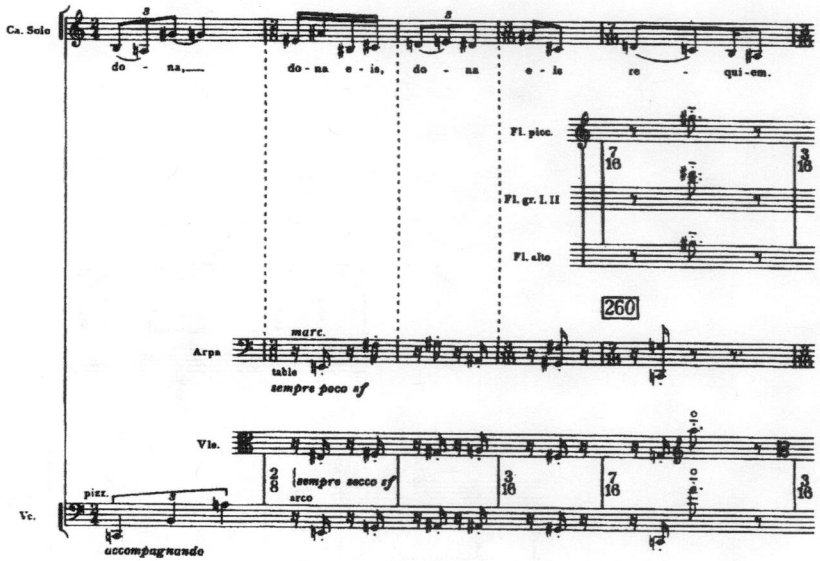
Ca. Solo
do - na,
do-na e - is,
do - na
e - is re - qui-em.
Fl. picc.
Fl. gr. I. II
Fl. alto
260
Arpa
marc.
table
sempre poco sf
Vla.
sempre secco sf
arco
pizz.
Vc.
accompagnando

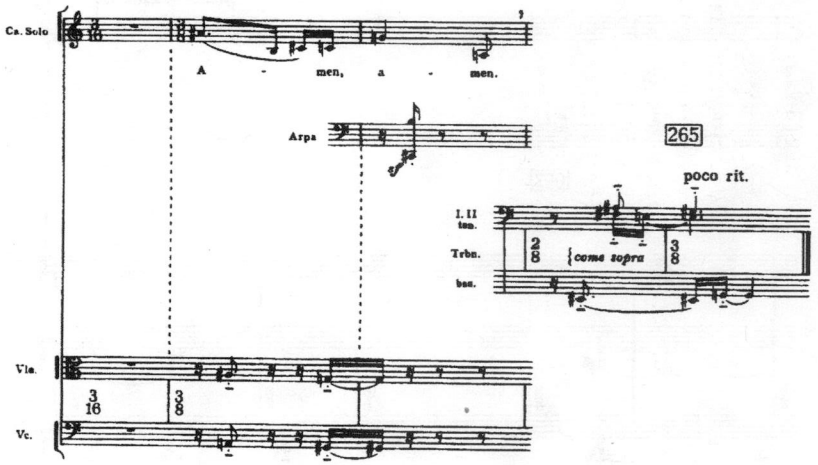
Ca. Solo
A - men, a - men.
Arpa
265
poco rit.
I. II ten.
Trbn.
bas.
come sopra
Vla.
Vc.

Translation of Text

On that day full of tears,
When from the ashes arises
Guilty man to be judged,
Spare him, O God.
Merciful Jesus, Lord,
Grant them eternal rest.
Amen.

25. Pierre Boulez (b. 1925)
Structures Ia, mm. 1-39 (1952)

Modéré, presque vif (♪ = 144)
mf subito
8
Modéré, presque vif (♪ = 144)
ppp subito
(mf)
12
(ppp)

fff subito
16
quasi f
(fff)
20
(quasi f)

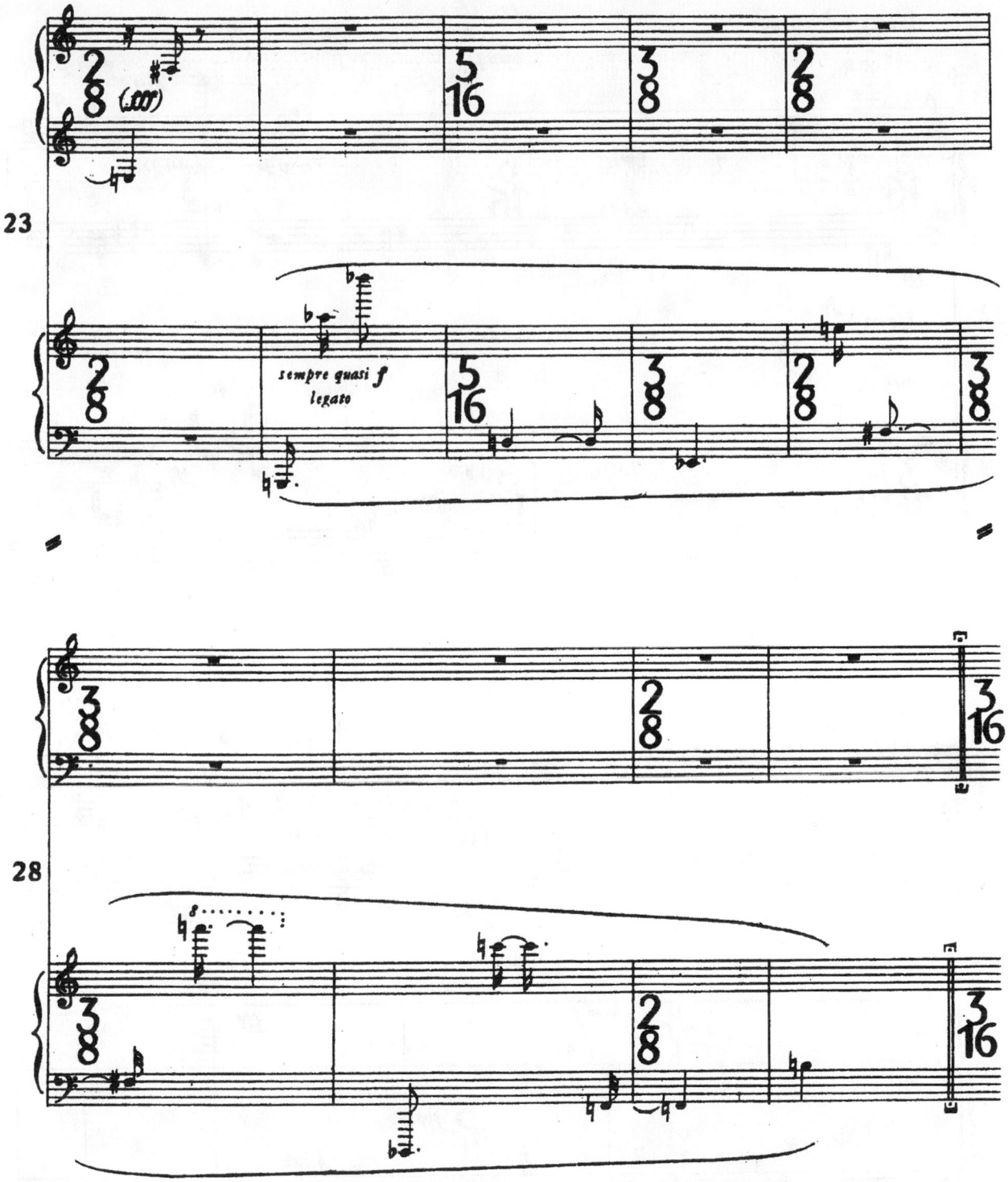
(ttr)
23
sempre quasi f
legato
28

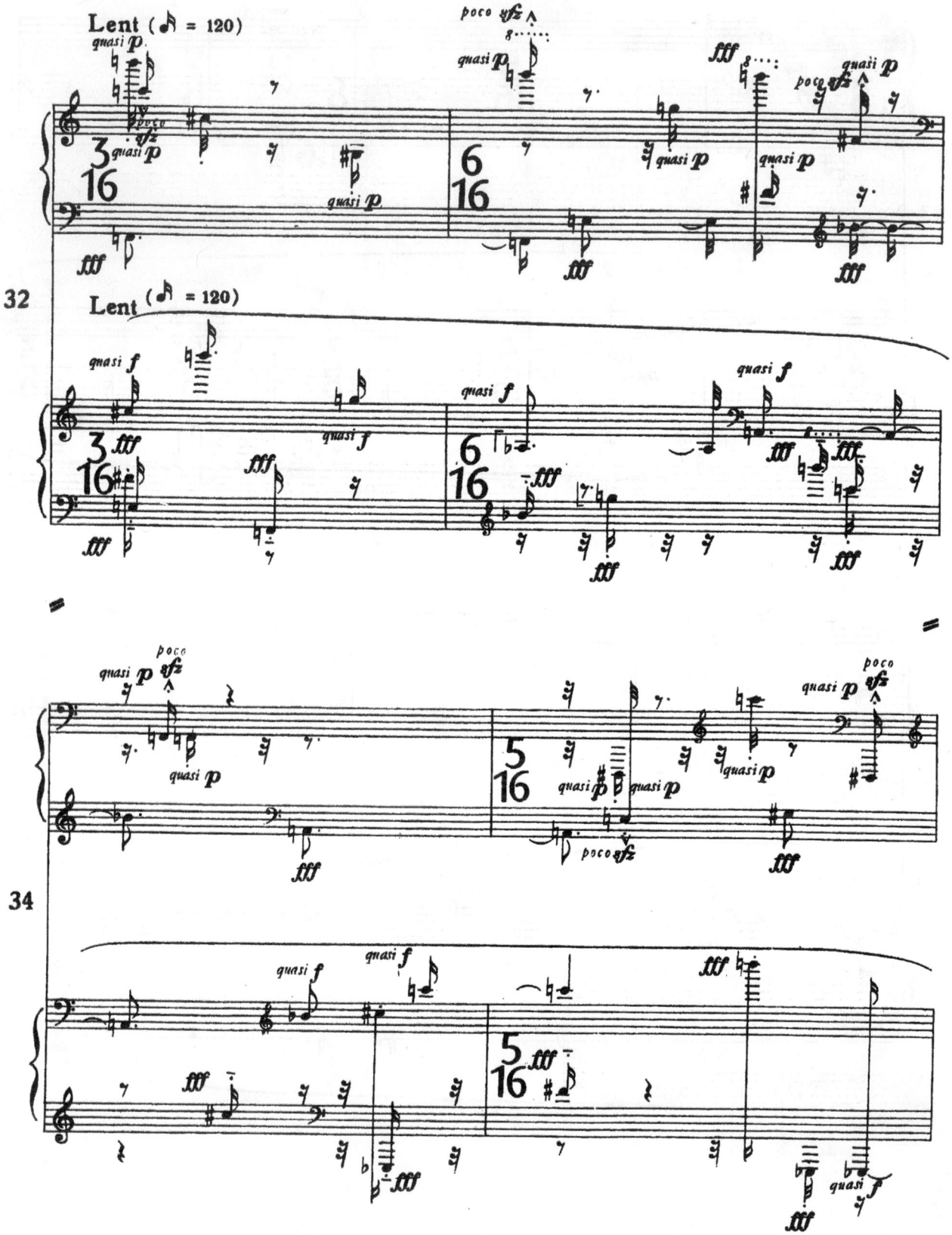
Lent (♪ = 120)
quasi p
poco sfz
fff
32
Lent (♪ = 120)
quasi f
34

36
quasi p
poco sfz
quasi p
quasi p
poco sfz
quasi p
quasi p
quasi p
quasi f
quasi f
quasi f
39
quasi p
poco sfz
quasi p
poco sfz
quasi p
poco sfz
quasi p
poco sfz
quasi f

26. Milton Babbitt (b. 1916)
Composition for Twelve Instruments, mm. 1-26 (1948)

6
3♩
2♩
(3♩)
Fl.
Ob.
Cl.
Bn.
Hn.
Tpt.
Hp.
Cel.
Vn.
Vla.
Vc.
B.
senza sord.
con sord.
senza sord.
(pizz.)

1
10
3
Fl.
Ob.
Cl.
Bn.
Hn.
Tpt.
Hp.
Cel.
senza sord.
con sord.
1
3
Vn.
Vla.
Vc.
B.
senza sord.
con sord.
arco

14
2♩
3♩
Fl.
Ob.
Cl.
Bn.
Hn.
Tpt.
(con sord.)
Hp.
Cel.
Vn.
Vla.
Vc.
B.

19
2
Fl.
Ob.
f
Cl.
pp
Bn.
mf<f
p — mf > pp
Hn.
p>pp
Tpt.
(con sord.)
p
Hp.
Cel.
mp
mf
2
Vn.
f — mf
Vla.
p<mp
(con sord.)
sul tasto
mf<ff — mp
Vc.
mp pp
B.
pizz.
mp

23
Fl.
Ob.
Cl.
Bn.
Hn.
Tpt.
Hp.
Cel.
Vn.
Vla.
Vc.
B.
mp > p
mp > p
f < ff
f < ff
(con sord.)
f > mp < f
mf
f
con sord.
mp > pp < mp
ord.
p < mp
con sord.
mp < mf
senza sord.
ff > f
(pizz.)
ff

27. Olivier Messiaen (1908-1992)

Turangalîla Symphony, Introduction, reh. 12-22 (1946-48)

2 Htb.
C. angl.
2 Clar. Si♭
Cl. basse Si♭
4 Cors Fa
1. et 3.
2. et 4.
Pte Trp. Ré
3 Trp. Ut
Cornet Si♭
3 Trbon.
Maracas
W. bl.
Caisse cl.
Cymb. ch.
Cloches
Piano
1ers Vons
2ds Vons Div.
Altos Div.
Velles
C.B.

13
Pte Fl.
2 Fl.
2 Htb.
C. angl.
2 Clar. Si♭
Cl. basse Si♭
3 Bons
Tuba
Trgl.
Caisse cl. Cymb. ch.
Célesta
Timbres
Vibr.
(sec) f
Piano
Onde
(son tournant)
8va bassa
13
1ers vons Div.
2ds vons Div.
Altos Div.
Div. (arco)
martelé f sec
Div. (pizz.)
C.B.

2 Fl.
2 Htb.
C.angl.
2 Clar. Sib
Cl. basse Sib
3 Bons
4 Cors Fa
1. et 3.
2. et 4.
pte Trp. Re
3 Trp. Ut
Cornet Sib
Trgl.
W. bl.
Marac.
Caisse cl.
Cymb. ch.
Cloches
Célesta
Timbres
Vibr.
Piano
Onde
1ers vons Div.
2ds vons Div.
Altos Div.
velles
C. B.

14
Pte Fl.
2 Fl.
2 Htb.
C. angl.
2 Clar. Sib
Cl. basse Sib
3 Buns
4 Cors Fa
Pte Trp. Re
3 Trp. Ut
Cornet Sib
3 Trbon
Tuba
Trgl. W bl.
Caisse cl. Cymb. ch.
Cloches
Célesta
Timbres
Vibr.
Piano
Onde
(son tournant)
8va bassa
14
1ers vons Div.
2ds vons Div.
Altos Div.
Div (arco)
Velles
martelé
Div. (pizz.)
C.B.

2 Htb.
C.angl.
2 Clar.
Sib
Cl.basse
Sib
4 Cors
Fa
1.et 3.
2.et 4.
Pte Trp.
Ré
3 Trp.
Ut
Cornet
Sib
3 Trbon.
W.bl.
Marac.
Caisse cl.
Cymb.ch.
Cloches
Piano
Altos
Div.
C.B.

15
Pte Fl.
2 Fl.
2 Htb.
C.angl.
2 Clar. Sib
Cl. basse Sib
3 Bons
4 Cors Fa
Pte Trp. Ré
3 Trp. Ut
Cornet Sib
3 Trbon.
W. bl. Marac.
Caisse cl. Cymb. ch.
Cloches
Célesta
Timbres
Vibr.
Piano
Ped.
Onde
(son tournant)
8va bassa
15
1ers vons Div.
2ds vons Div.
Altos Div.
Div. (arco)
martelé
velles
C.B.
Div. (pizz.)

2 Htb.
C.angl.
2 Clar.
Si♭
Cl. basse
Si♭
4 Cors
Fa
1. et 3.
2. et 4.
Pte Trp.
Ré
3 Trp.
Ut
Cornet
Si♭
W. bl.
Marac.
Caisse cl.
Cymb. ch.
Cloches
Piano
Ped.
1ers vons
2ds vons
Div.
Altos
Div.
velles
C.B.

16
Pte Fl.
2 Fl.
2 Hb.
C.angl.
2 Clar. Sib
Cl. basse Sib
3 Bons
4 Cors Fa
Pte Trp. Re
3 Trp. Ut
Cornet Sib
3 Trbon.
Tuba
Trgl. W. bl.
W. bl.
Caisse cl. Cymb. ch.
Cloches
Célesta
Timbres
Vibr.
Piano
Onde
(son tournant)
8va bassa
16
1ers vons Div.
2ds vons Div.
Altos Div.
Div. (arco) martelé
Velles
Div. (pizz.)
C.B

17
Pte Fl.
2 Fl.
2 Htb.
C. angl.
2 Clar.
Sib
Cl. basse
Sib
3 Bons
4 Cors
Fa
Pte Trp.
Ré
3 Trp.
Ut
Cornet
Sib
3 Trbon.
W. bl.
Marac.
Caisse cl.
Cymb. ch.
Cloches
Célesta
Timbres
Vibr.
Piano
Onde
(son tournant)
8va bassa
17
Div.
Div.
Altos
Div.
Div. (arco) martelé
Div. (pizz.)
C.B.

Pte Fl.
2 Fl.
2 Hb.
C. angl.
2 Clar. Sib
Cl. basse Sib
3 Bons
4 Cors Fa
Pte Trp Ré
3 Trp Ut
Cornet Sib
Tuba
Trgl.
W. bl.
Marac.
Caisse cl.
Cymb ch.
Cloches
Célesta
Timbres
Vibr.
Piano
Onde
Div.
Div.
Altos
Div.
Violles
C.B.
Trgl.
W. bl.
Marac.
W. bl.
pp
mf
pp
mf
Ped.
*

18
2 Hb.
C.angl.
2 Clar.
Sib
Cl. basse
Sib
4 Cors
Fa
Pte Trp.
Ré
3 Trp.
Ut
Cornet
Sib
Trgl.
W. bl.
Marac.
Marac.
W. bl.
Caisse cl.
Cymb ch.
Cloches
Piano
Ped.
18
1ers vons
2ds vons
Div.
Altos
Div.
velles
C.B.

Pte Fl.
2 Fl.
2 Htb.
C. angl.
2 Clar. Si♭
Cl. basse Si♭
3 Bons
4 Cors Fa
Pte Trp. Ré
3 Trp. Ut
Cornet Si♭
3 Trbon.
Tuba
Trgl.
W. bl.
Marac.
Caisse cl.
Cymb. ch.
Célesta
Timbres
Vibr
Piano
Onde
(son tournant)
8va basso
1ers vons Div.
2ds vons Div.
Altos Div.
Div. (arco)
martelé
Velles
Div. (pizz.)
C.B.

19
Pte Fl.
2 Fl.
2 Htb.
C. angl.
2 Clar. Si♭
Cl. basse Si♭
3 Bons
4 Cors Fa
Pte Trp. Ré
3 Trp. Ut
Cornet Si♭
Tuba
Trgl.
W. bl.
Marac.
Caisse cl.
Cymb.ch.
Cloches
Célesta
Timbres
Vibr.
Piano
Onde
1ers vons Div.
2ds vons Div.
Altos Div.
Velles
C.B.

2 Htb.
C. angl.
2 Clar. Si♭
Cl. basse Si♭
4 Cors Fa
P^le Trp. Ré
3 Trp. Ut
Cornet Si♭
W. bl.
Marac.
Caisse cl.
Cymb. ch.
Cloches
Piano
1ers Vons
2^ds Vons Div.
Altos Div.
f
mf
pp
Ped.

20
2 Hb.
C. angl.
2 Clar. Sib
Cl. basse Sib
4 Cors Fa
Pte Trp. Re
3 Trp. Ut
Cornet Sib
3 Trbon.
Marac.
W. bl.
W. bl. Marac.
Caisse cl. Cymb. ch.
Cloches
Piano
Ped.
20
1ers Vons
2 ds Vons Div.
Altos Div.
Velles
C B.

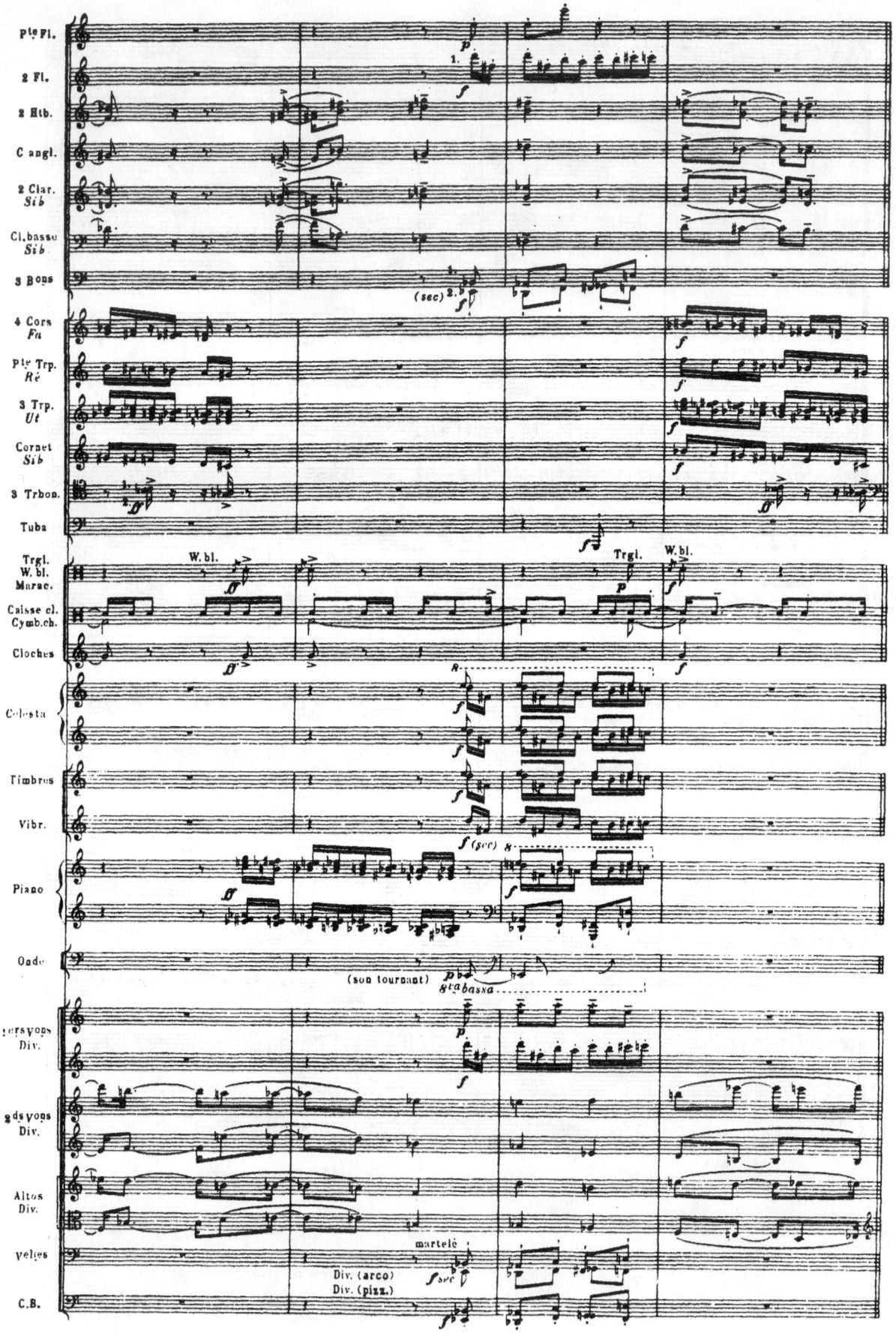
Pte Fl.
2 Fl.
2 Htb.
C angl.
2 Clar. Sib
Cl. basse Sib
3 Bons
(sec)
4 Cors Fa
Pte Trp. Ré
3 Trp. Ut
Cornet Sib
3 Trbon.
Tuba
Trgl.
W. bl.
Marac.
Caisse cl.
Cymb. ch.
Cloches
Trgl.
W. bl.
Celesta
Timbres
Vibr.
(sec)
Piano
Onde
(son tournant)
8va bassa
1ers vons Div.
2ds vons Div.
Altos Div.
Velles
martelé
Div. (arco)
Div. (pizz.)
C.B.

21
Presque lent (♪= 80)
Pte Fl.
2 Fl.
2 Htb.
C. angl.
2 Clar. Sib
Cl. basse Sib
3 Bons
4 Cors Fa
Pte Trp. Re
3 Trp. Ut
Cornet Sib
3 Trbon.
Tuba
Cymb. susp.
Cymb. susp.
Tam-tam
Timbres
21
Presque lent (♪= 80)
Piano
1ers violons
2ds violons Div.
Altos Div.
Velles Div.
C.B.

22 Un peu vif (♩ = 100)
Bien modéré (♪ = 92)
Pte Fl.
2 Fl.
2 Htb.
C.angl.
2 Clar. Si♭
Cl.basse Si♭
3 Bons
4 Cors Fa
Pte Trp. Ré
3 Trp. Ut
Cornet Si♭
3 Trbon.
Tuba
Cymb.susp.
W.bl.
Cymb.ch.
Tam-tam
Tam-tam
Gr.caisse
Cymb.chin.
rall.
Gr. Caisse
Timbres
Célesta
Piano
(Ruban-timbre Onde-A)
glissando
Onde
1ers vons
2 ds vons
Altos
velles
C.B

28. Elliott Carter (b. 1908)

String Quartet no. 2, I, mm. 35-134 (1959)

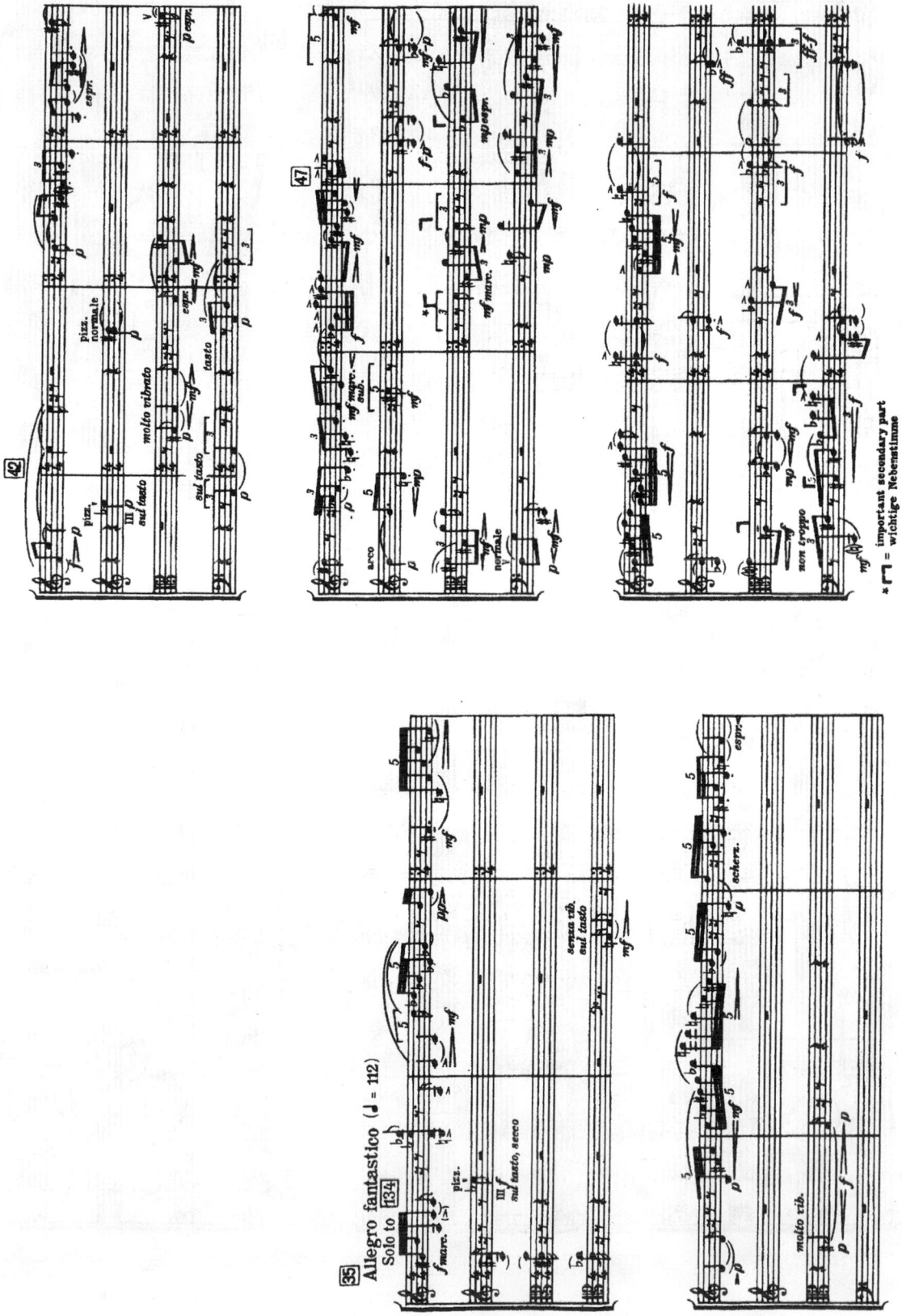

51
f mare.
p espr.

57
f mare.

♩ = ♫. = 112
♪ = ♪ (♪ = 186.7)

62
scherzando

68
pizz.
f mare.
arco
in fuori
f espr.
poco
cresc. molto f non troppo mp

71
mare.

75
(♩ = 140)
leggiero
pp leggiero
in fuori
80
ben in fuori /

mf marc.
cant.
85
mp ben cant.
(♩ = 140)
89

94
sub.
marc.
(p sempre)
f sub.
98
= 70
(163.3)
p tranquillo
pizz.

105
arco
p tranquillo
pp leggiero
110
gliss.
détaché

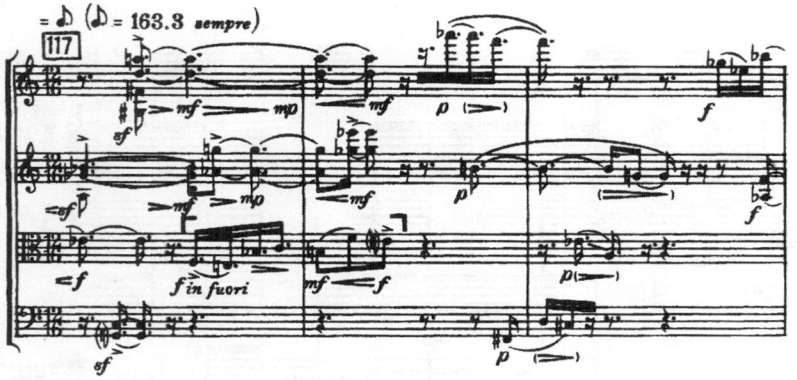
= ♪ (♪ = 163.3 sempre)
117
mf
mp
p
f
sf
f in fuori

123
mf
mp
f
mp sub.
espr.
in fuori
f cant. espr.

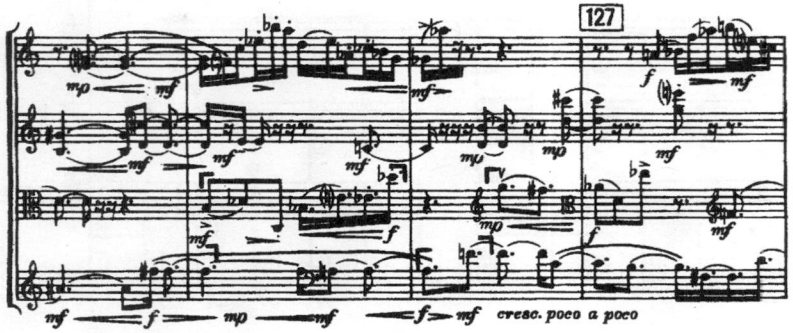
127
mf
f
mp
cresc. poco a poco

130
ff
p sub.
ff sub.
pp
p

♪ =
ff
f
p
mp
pp
mf
molto espr.
attacca

29. Karlheinz Stockhausen (b. 1928)

Stimmung (three pages: *Formschema*, one sample page of *Modelle*, and one sample page of *Magische Namen*) (1968)

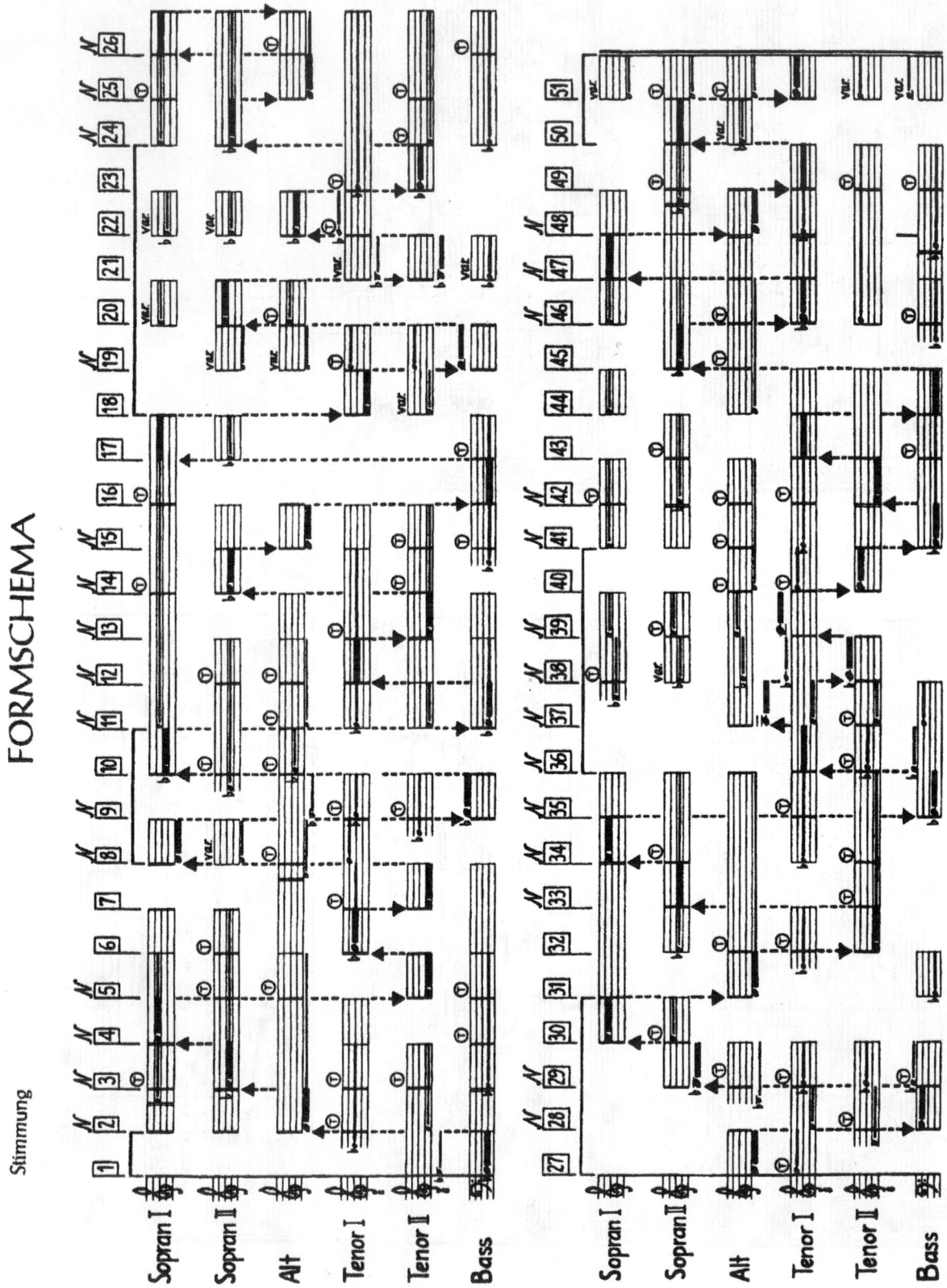

Stockhausen
STIMMUNG

Modelle

Männerstimme

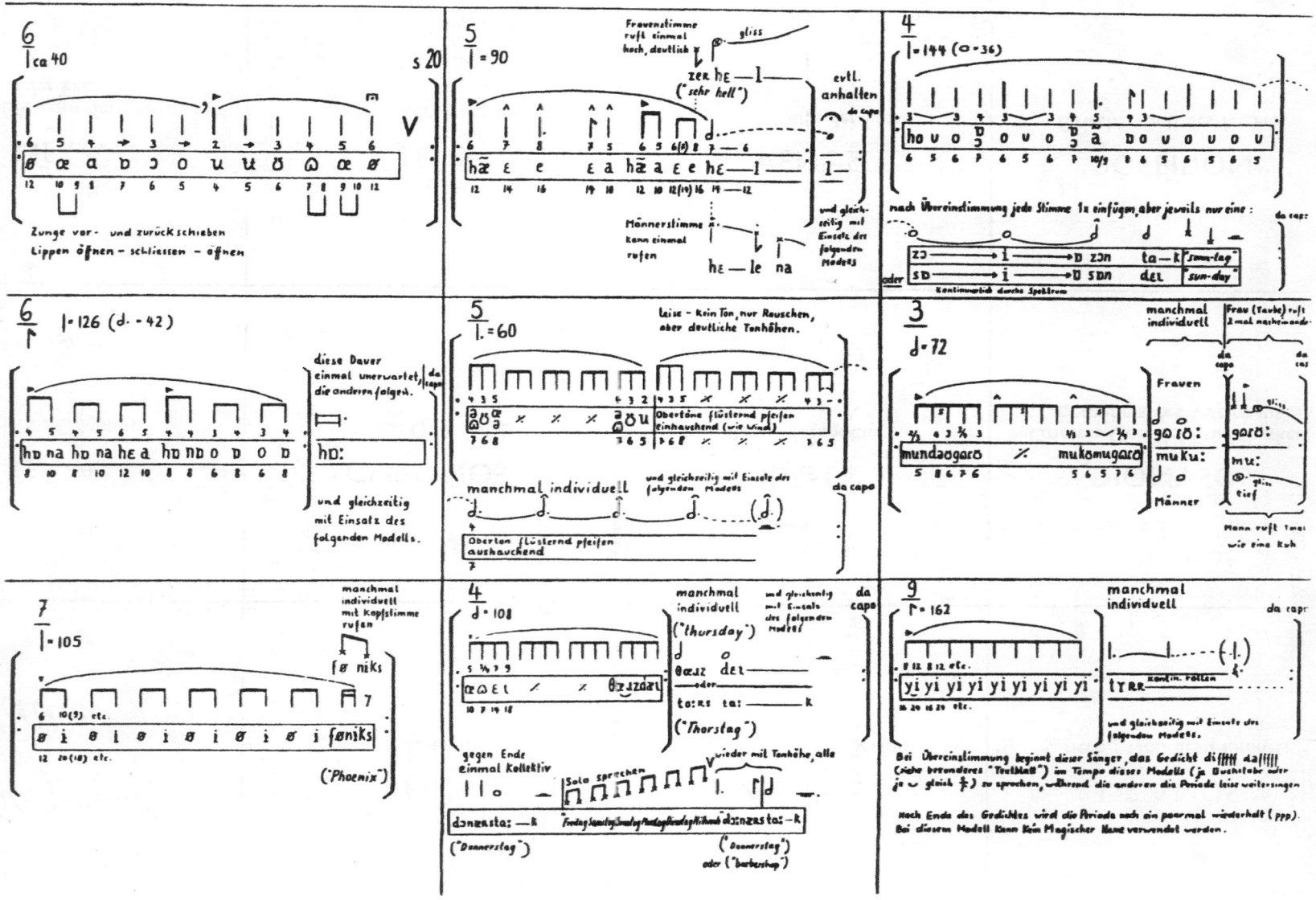

Magische Namen	RHEA Griech.: Mutter von Zeus	AEOLUS Griech.: Gott der Winde	URANOS Griech.: Gott des Himmels
GAIA Griech.: Erdgöttin	CHRONOS Griech.: Gott der Zeit	DIANA Röm.: Jagdgöttin	DIONYSOS Griech.: Gott der Fruchtbarkeit, besonders des Weinbaus
HERA Griech.: Beschützerin der Frauen und der Ehe	ZEUS Griech.: König der Götter	VENUS Röm.: Göttin der Liebe	POSEIDON Griech.: Gott des Meeres

30. John Cage (1912-1992)
Winter Music (one page) (1957)

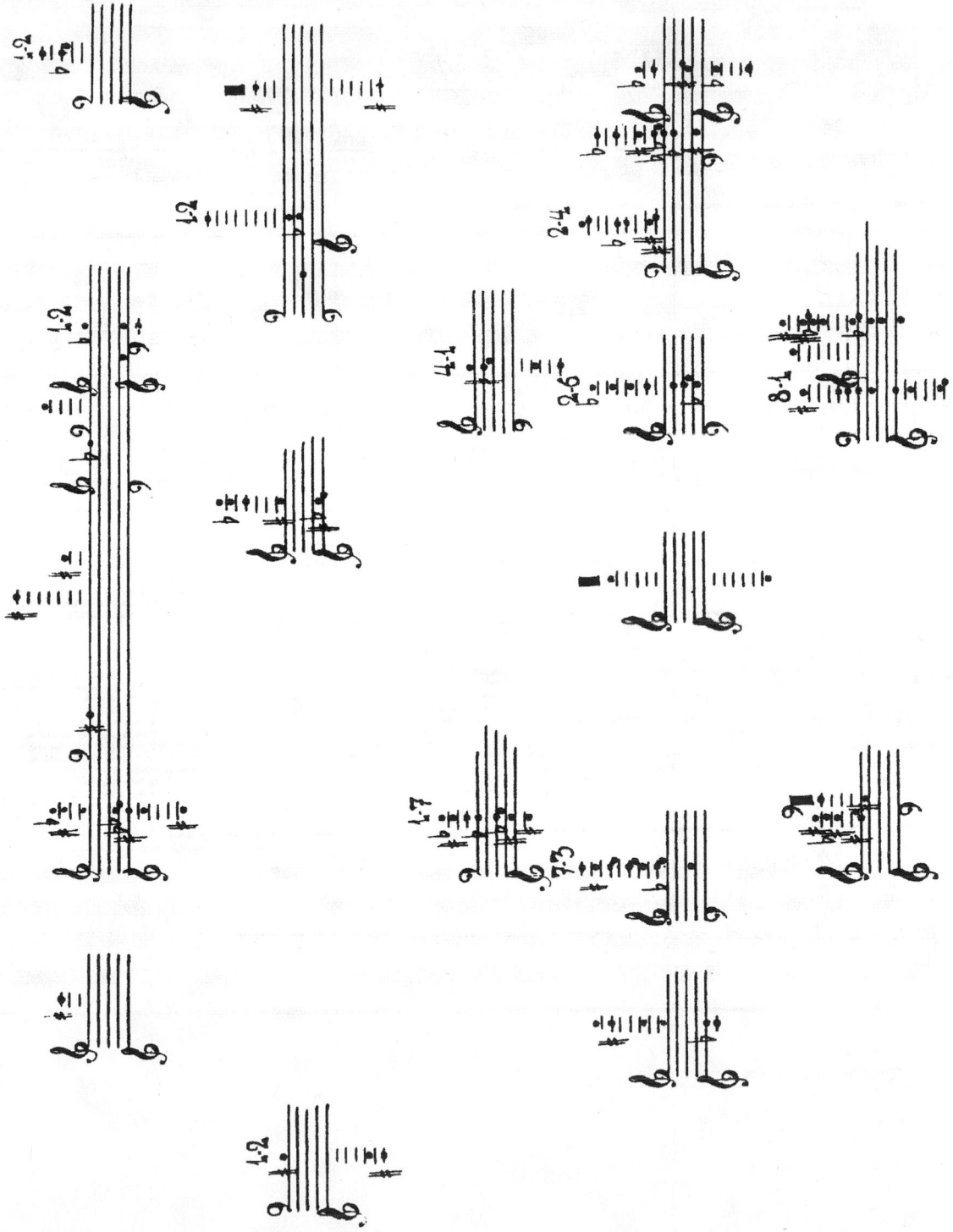

31. Witold Lutosławski (1913-1994)
Jeux vénitiens, I (1960-61)

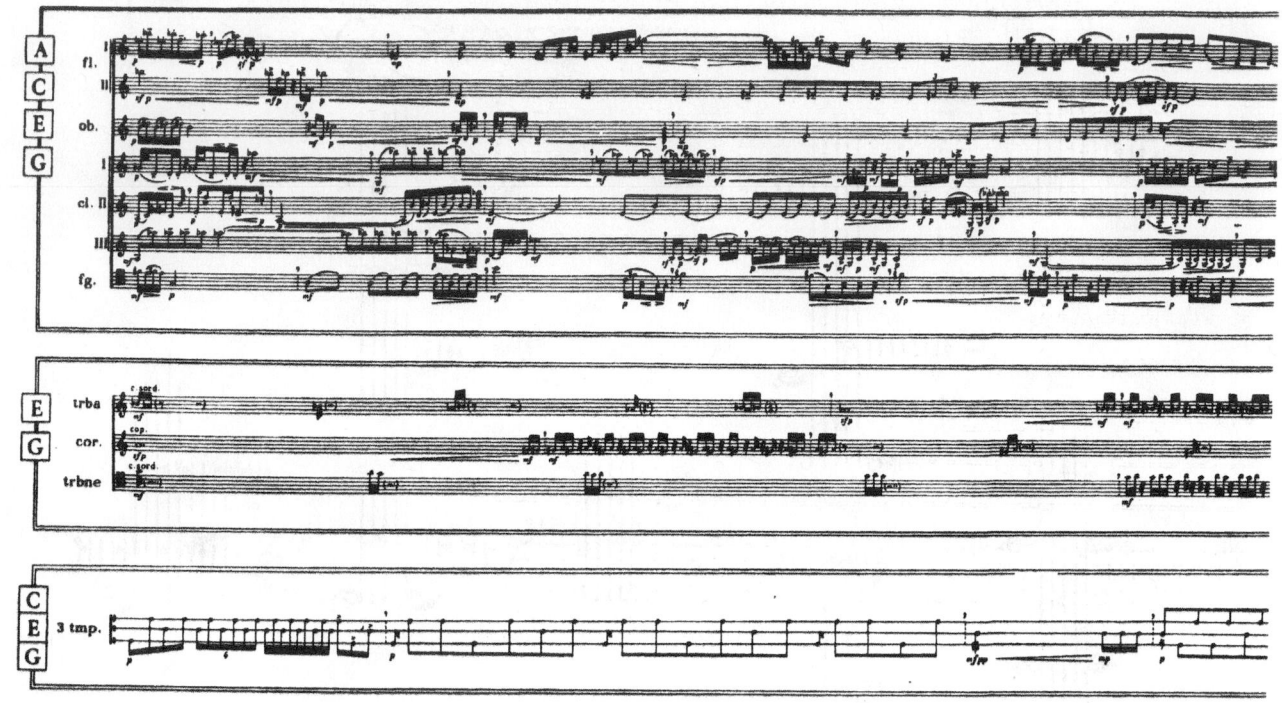

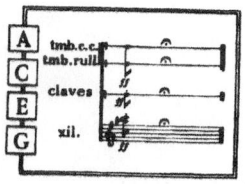

Kolejność wykonania A B C D E F G H

Odcinki A C E G:

A – gra grupa instrumentów dętych drewnianych i perkusji;

C – instrumenty dęte drewniane, kotły i perkusja;

E – instrumenty dęte drewniane i blaszane, kotły i perkusja;

G – instrumenty dęte drewniane i blaszane, kotły, perkusja i fortepian.

Przerywane „kreski taktowe" ze znakiem cezury oznaczają cezurę o dowolnym czasie trwania. Zależnie od długości cezur faktura brzmieniowa będzie bardziej zwarta lub bardziej rozrzedzona.

Czas trwania poszczególnych odcinków: A = 12", C = 18", E = 6", G = 24". Dyrygent daje znak na rozpoczęcie i zakończenie każdego odcinka (znak na zakończenie odcinka A jest równocześnie znakiem na rozpoczęcie odcinka B, koniec odcinka C to zarazem początek odcinka D itd.). Przy znaku na zakończenie odcinka muzycy powinni natychmiast przerwać grę. Jeżeli muzyk ukończył już swoją partię wcześniej, powinien ją powtarzać od początku. Następne odcinki, oznaczone kolejno literami C, E, G, nie powinny być grane od początku, poszczególni wykonawcy rozpoczynają od jakiejkolwiek innej frazy między dwiema cezurami.

Każdy muzyk wykonuje swoją partię tak swobodnie, jakby grał sam.

Wartości rytmiczne są podane orientacyjnie, tempo podstawowe waha się między 140 a 150 = ♩

Odcinki B D F H:

Kreski taktowe, wartości rytmiczne i metrum mają znaczenie jedynie orientacyjne. Muzyka ma być odtworzona jak najswobodniej. Ilość nut w miejscach podobnych do 3 taktu I altówki (B) zależy od siły pociągnięcia smyczkiem (smyczkiem skaczącym lub raczej ricochetem). W odcinku D partia skrzypiec powinna być wykonana niezależnie od dyrygenta i reszty zespołu.

Order of performance: A B C D E F G H

Sections A C E G:

A is played by the wood winds and percussion group; C by the wood winds, kettledrums, and percussion; E by the wood winds, brass, kettledrums, and percussion; G by the wood winds, brass, kettledrums, percussion, and piano. The broken "bar lines" with a caesura above call for a caesura of optional length; on the length of the caesura will depend the density of the texture.

Duration of the particular sections: A = 12", C = 18" E = 6", G = 24". The conductor gives the sign for the beginning and end of each section (the beat showing the end of section A also indicates the beginning of section B, the beat showing the end of C, the beginning of D, etc.). When the sign for the end of each section is given, the performers must interrupt playing immediately. If by this time a player has already played his part to the end, he should repeat it from the beginning of the section. In the following sections, which are indicated by the letters in the order C, E, G, the individual parts

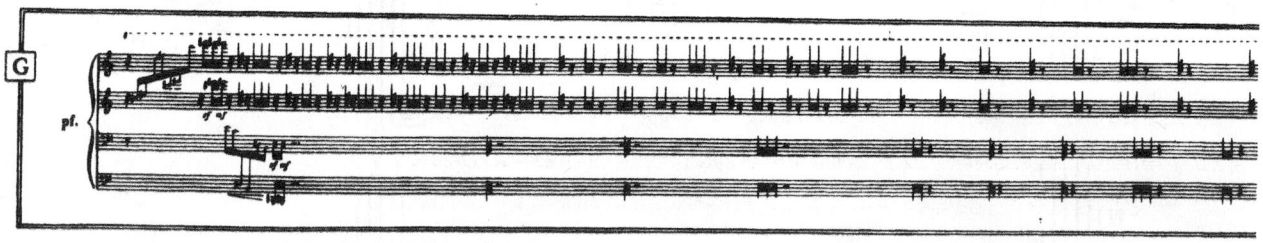

N.B.: All instruments in this score are notated in C.

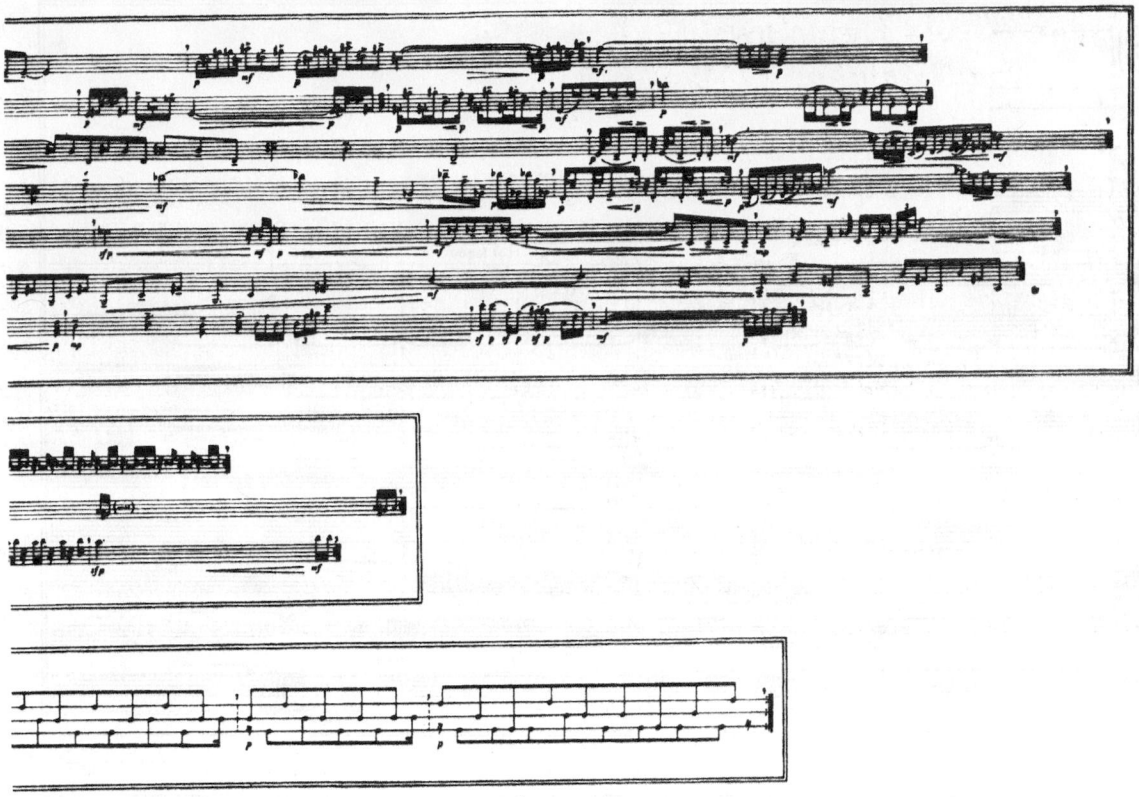

ought not to be played from the beginning but from any other phrase between two caesuras. Each musician should play his part with the same freedom as if he were playing it alone; the rhythmic values serve only as a guide and the basic tempo is between ♪ = 140 and ♪ = 150.

Sections B D F H:

The bar lines, rhythmical values, and metre are intended merely for orientation; the music should be played with the greatest possible freedom. The number of notes at places like the third bar of section B in the first viola part depends on the strength of the player's bowing (*spiccato* or preferably *ricochet*). In section D the first violin part should be played independently of the conductor and the rest of the ensemble.

Reihenfolge der Wiedergabe: A B C D E F G H

Abschnitte A C E G:

A wird von der Holzbläser- und Schlagzeuggruppe gespielt; C von Holzbläsern, Pauken und Schlagzeug; E von Holzbläsern und Blechbläsern, Pauken und Schlagzeug; G von Holzbläsern, Blechbläsern, Pauken, Schlagzeug und Klavier. Die durchbrochenen „Taktstriche" mit Zäsurzeichen darüber verlangen Zäsuren von beliebiger Dauer; je nach Dauer der Zäsuren wird das Klangbild dichter oder lockerer erscheinen. Spieldauer der einzelnen Abschnitte: A = 12", C = 18", E = 6," G = 24". Der Dirigent gibt die Zeichen für Beginn und Schluß eines jeden Abschnittes (der Abschlag für Abschnitt A gilt gleichzeitig als Einsatz für B, der Abschlag für C als Einsatz für D usw.).

Beim Abschlag eines jeden Abschnittes sollen die Musiker ihr Spiel sofort unterbrechen. Hat ein Musiker einen entsprechenden Part bereits vor diesem Zeitpunkt beendet, wiederholt er ihn vom Beginn des betreffenden Abschnitts an. Die folgenden Abschnitte, nacheinander durch Buchstaben C E G bezeichnet, sind so zu verstehen, daß die einzelnen Stimmen nicht von Anfang an sondern von irgendeiner anderen Phrase zwischen zwei Zäsuren gespielt werden sollen. Jeder Musiker führt seinen Part so frei aus, als ob er ihn allein spiele; die rhythmischen Werte dienen nur als Anhalt; das Grundtempo liegt zwischen ♪ = 140 und ♪ = 150.

Abschnitte B D F H:

Taktstriche, rhythmische Werte und Metrum dienen lediglich als Orientierungshilfen, die Musik soll so frei wie möglich gespielt werden. Die Anzahl der Noten an ähnlichen Stellen wie im 3. Takt (B) der Viola I hängt von der Kraft des Bogenstriches ab (mit Springbogen oder besser *ricochet*). Im Abschnitt D soll die I. Violine ihren Part unabhängig vom Dirigenten und dem übrigen Ensemble spielen.

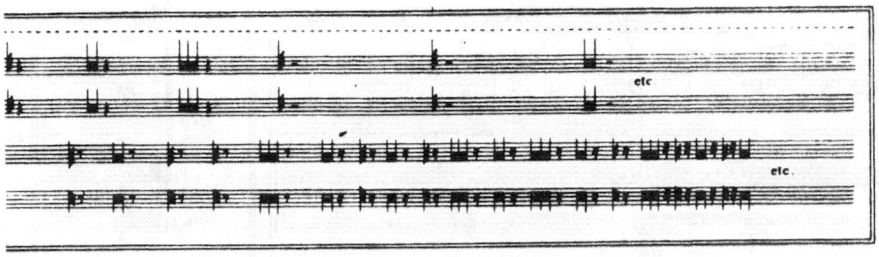

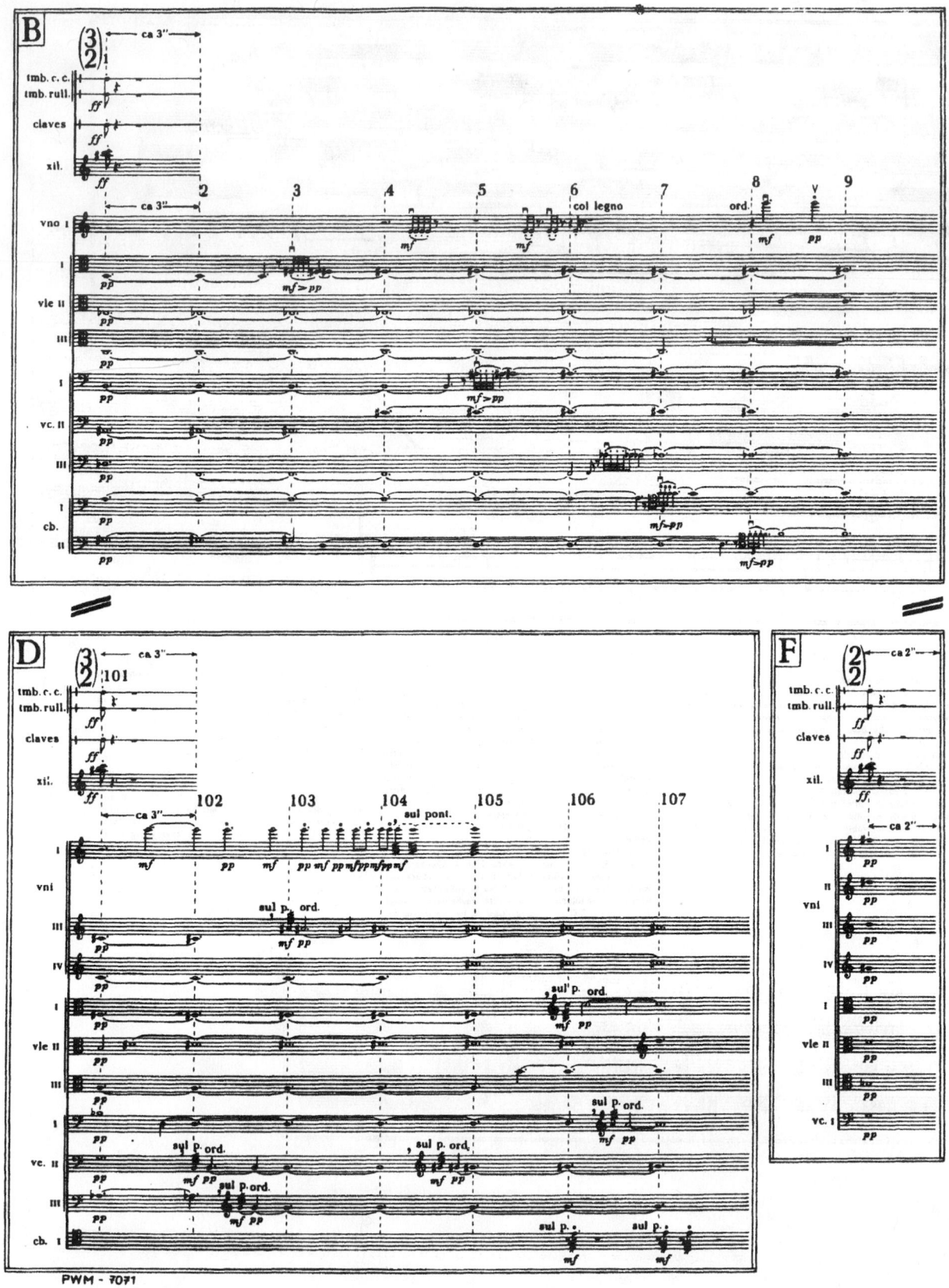
B
ca 3"
tmb. c. c.
tmb. rull.
claves
xil.
vno I
vle II
vc. II
cb.
col legno
ord.
D
101
102
103
104
105
106
107
sul pont.
sul p. ord.
vni
vle II
vc. II
cb. I
PWM - 7071
F
ca 2"
vc. I

H
ca 3"
tmb. c. c.
tmb. rull.
claves
xil.
vni
vle II
vc.
sul p.
pizz.
vle
vc. I

32. György Ligeti (1923-2006)

Ramifications, mm. 1-44 (1968-69)

*) The instruments in Group I sound a quarter-tone higher than written.

* *) Double bass: it is written in the usual octave transposition, with exception of the natural harmonics, which are written as they sound („SUONI REALI"). Concerning the artificial harmonics: their touch is written in the octave transposition, their resulting tone as it sounds.

*) Die Instrumente in Gruppe I klingen einen Vierteltonhöher als notiert.

* *) Kontrabaß: in der üblichen Oktaventransposition notiert mit Ausnahme der natürlichen Flageoletts, die wie notiert klingen ("SUONI REALI"). Was die künstlichen Flageoletts betrifft, ist die Griffschrift in der Oktav-Transposition notiert, der sich aus ihr ergebende Ton so wie er klingt.

3
4
I. Gruppe (Einen Viertelton höher)
I. Group (A Quarter-tone higher)
Vn. 1
Vn. 3
Vn. 5
Vn. 7
Vl. 1
Vc. 1
IV. V tenuto senza vibr.
ppp
II. V tenuto senza vibr.
ppp
II. Gruppe
II. Group
Vn. 2
Vn. 4
Vn. 6
Vl. 2
Vc. 2
Cb.

5
6
I. Group (A Quarter-tone higher)
Vn. 1
Vn. 3
Vn. 5
Vn. 7
Vl. 1
Vc. 1
II. Group
Vn. 2
Vn. 4
Vn. 6
Vl. 2
Vc.
Cb.
Tutti
suono reale
II. V
tenuto, senza vibr.
ppp

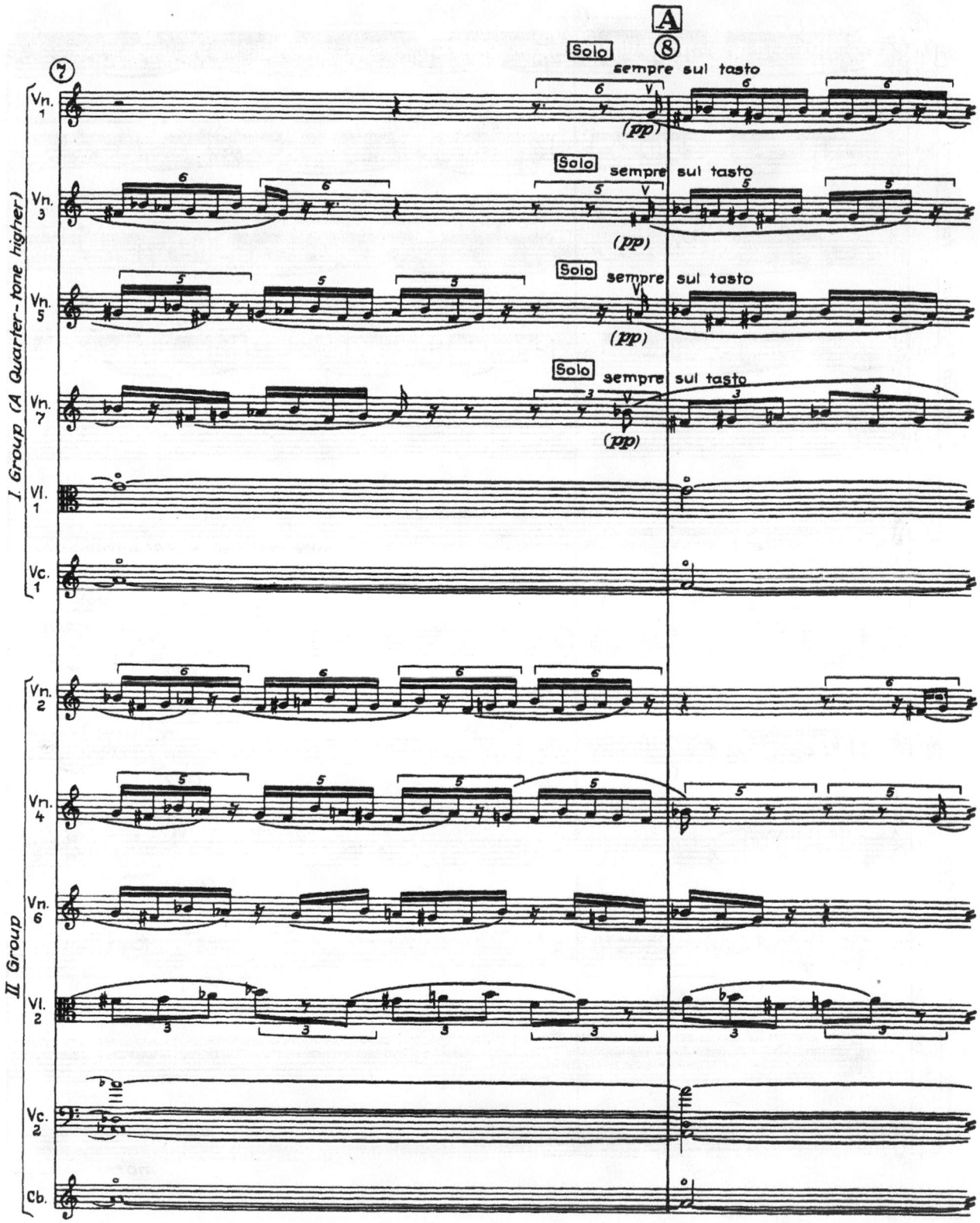
A
7
8
Solo
sempre sul tasto
(pp)
I. Group (A Quarter-tone higher)
II Group
Vn. 1
Vn. 3
Vn. 5
Vn. 7
Vl. 1
Vc. 1
Vn. 2
Vn. 4
Vn. 6
Vl. 2
Vc. 2
Cb.

9
I. Group (A Quarter-tone higher)
Vn. 1
Vn. 3
Vn. 5
Vn. 7
Vl. 1
Vc. 1
morendo - - - - al niente
II. Group
Vn. 2
Solo
(sempre sul tasto)
(pp)
Vn. 4
Solo
(sempre sul tasto)
(pp)
Vn. 6
Solo
(sempre sul tasto)
(pp)
Vl. 2
Solo
(sempre sul tasto)
(pp)
Vc. 2
Cb.
morendo - -

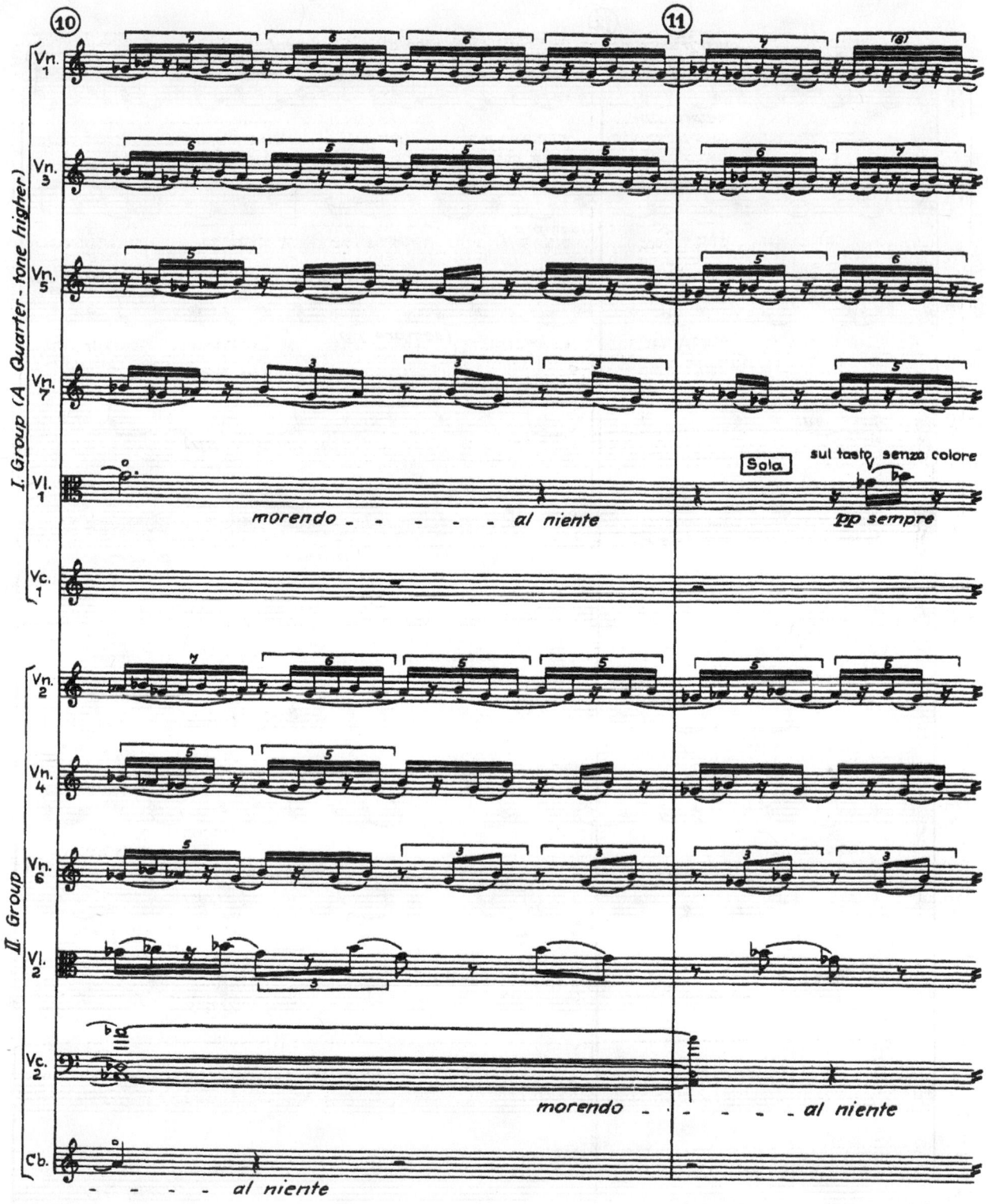
10
11
I. Group (A Quarter-tone higher)
Vn. 1
Vn. 3
Vn. 5
Vn. 7
Vl. 1
Vc. 1
Sola
sul tasto, senza colore
morendo - - - - - al niente
pp sempre
II. Group
Vn. 2
Vn. 4
Vn. 6
Vl. 2
Vc. 2
Cb.
morendo - - - - - al niente
- - - - - al niente

12
poco a poco ord. - - - - poco a poco sul pont.
(sempre pp)
poco a poco ord. - - - - poco a poco sul pont.
(sempre pp)
poco a poco ord. - - - - poco a poco sul
(sempre pp)
poco a poco ord. - - - -
(sempre pp)
poco a
Vn. 1
Vn. 3
Vn. 5
Vn. 7
Vl. 1
Vc. 1
I. Group (A Quarter-tone higher)
Vn. 2
Vn. 4
Vn. 6
Vl. 2
Vc. 2
Cb.
II Group

13
14
I. Group (A Quarter-tone higher)
II. Group
Vn. 1
Vn. 3
Vn. 5
Vn. 7
Vl. 1
Vc. 1
Vn. 2
Vn. 4
Vn. 6
Vl. 2
Vc. 2
Cb.
pont.
poco a poco sul pont.
poco ord. - - - - poco a poco sul pont.
(sempre pp)
poco a poco ord. - - - - poco a poco sul pont.
(sempre pp)
poco a poco ord. - - - - poco a poco sul pont.
(sempre pp)
poco a poco ord. - - - - poco a poco sul pont.
(sempre pp)
poco a poco ord. - - - - poco
(sempre pp)

15
I. Group (A Quarter-tone higher)
Vn. 1
Vn. 3
Vn. 5
Vn. 7
Vl. 1
Vc. 1
ord.
ord.
ord.
II. Group
Vn. 2
Vn. 4
Vn. 6
Vl. 2
Vc. 2
Cb.
a poco sul pont.

B
16
17
I. Group (A Quarter-tone higher)
Vn. 1
Vn. 3
Vn. 5
Vn. 7
Vl. 1
Vc. 1
II Group
Vn. 2
Vn. 4
Vn. 6
Vl. 2
Vc. 2
Cb.
ord.
5
6
7

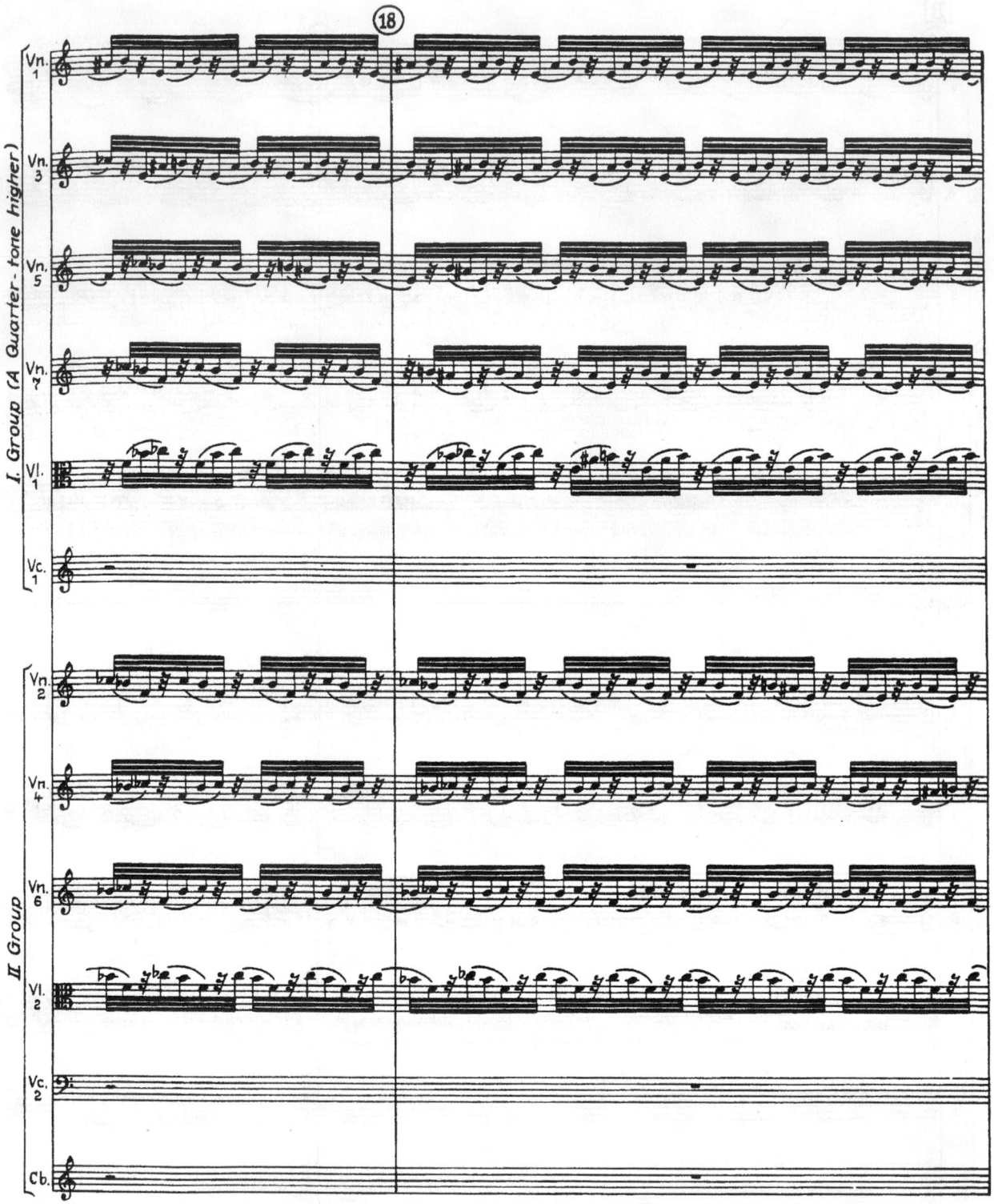
18
I. Group (A Quarter-tone higher)
Vn. 1
Vn. 3
Vn. 5
Vn. 7
Vl. 1
Vc. 1
II Group
Vn. 2
Vn. 4
Vn. 6
Vl. 2
Vc. 2
Cb.

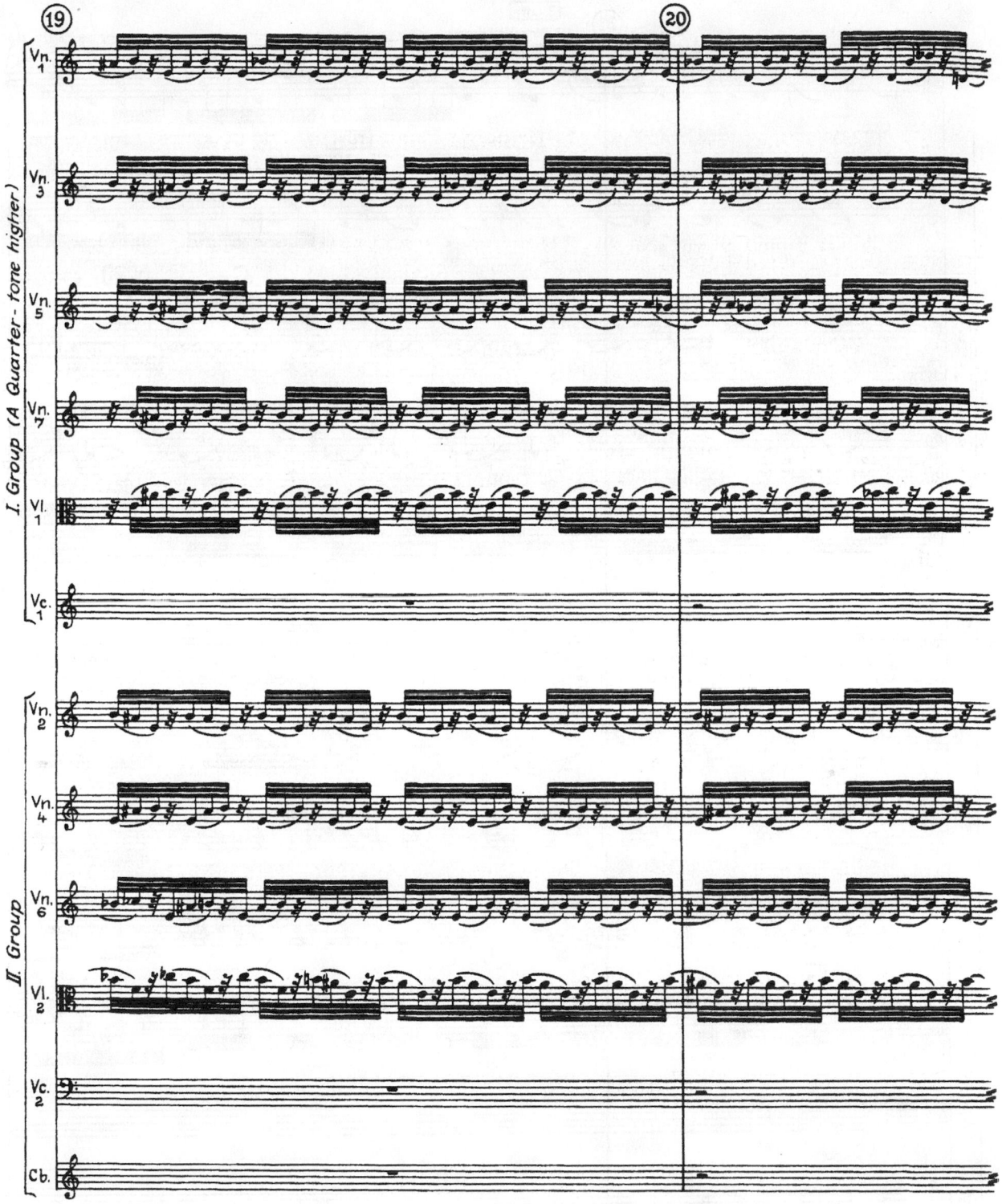
19
20
I. Group (A Quarter-tone higher)
Vn. 1
Vn. 3
Vn. 5
Vn. 7
Vl. 1
Vc. 1
II. Group
Vn. 2
Vn. 4
Vn. 6
Vl. 2
Vc. 2
Cb.

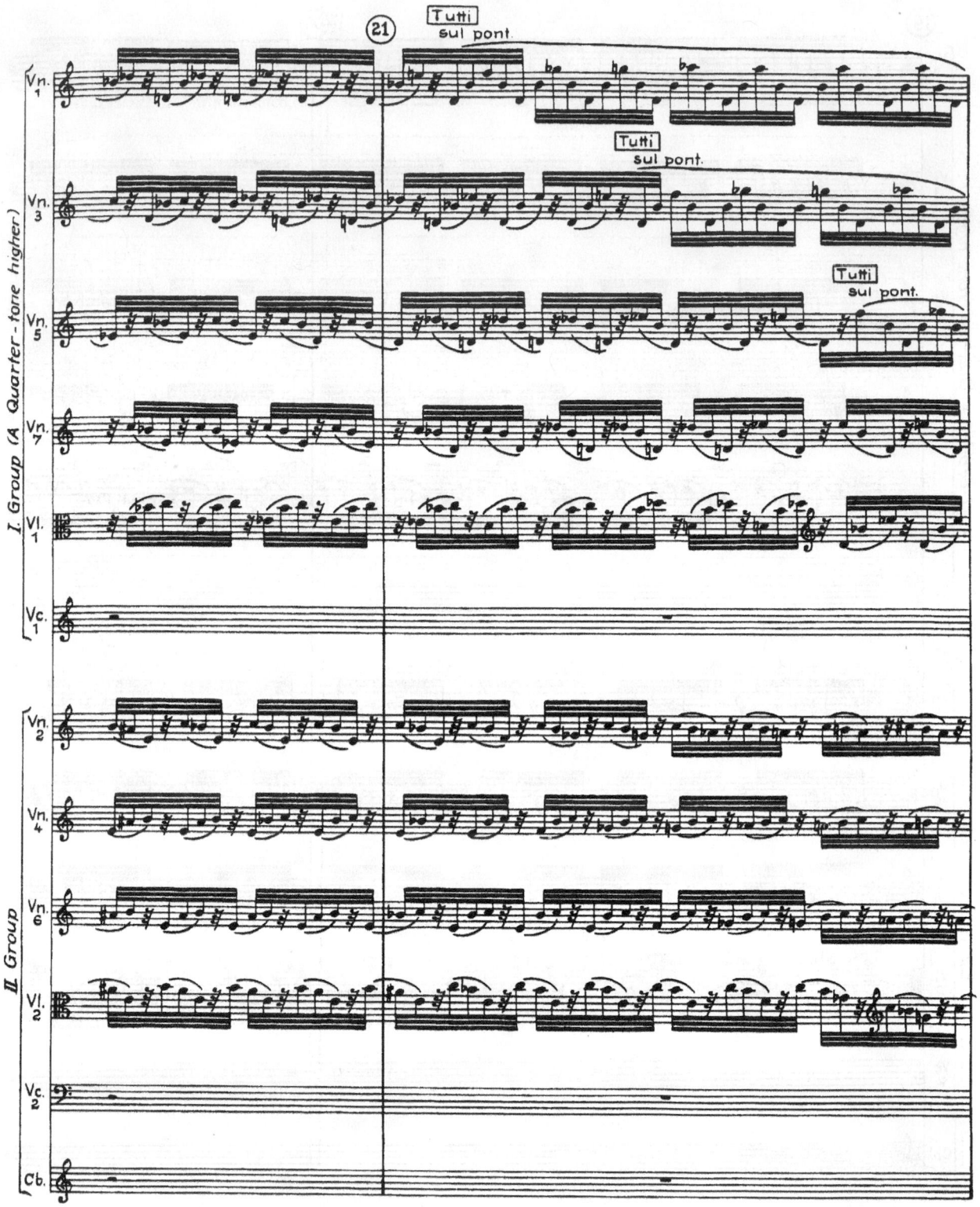
21
Tutti
sul pont.
Tutti
sul pont.
Tutti
sul pont.
I. Group (A Quarter-tone higher)
Vn. 1
Vn. 3
Vn. 5
Vn. 7
Vl. 1
Vc. 1
II Group
Vn. 2
Vn. 4
Vn. 6
Vl. 2
Vc. 2
Cb.

22
23
I Group (A Quarter-tone higher)
Vn. 1
Vn. 3
Vn. 5
Tutti
sul pont.
Vn. 7
Vl. 1
Vc. 1
II Group
Vn. 2
Tutti
sul pont.
Vn. 4
Vn. 6
Vl. 2
Vc. 2
Cb.

24
I. Group (A Quarter-tone higher)
Vn. 1
Vn. 3
Vn. 5
Vn. 7
Tutte
sul pont.
Vl. 1
Vc. 1
II Group
Vn. 2
Tutti
sul pont.
Vn. 4
Tutti
sul pont.
Vn. 6
Tutte
sul pont.
Vl. 2
Vc. 2
Cb.

C
25
26
I. Group (A Quarter-tone higher)
Vn. 1
Vn. 3
Vn. 5
Vn. 7
Vl. 1
Vc. 1
poco a poco ord.
II. Group
Vn. 2
Vn. 4
Vn. 6
Vl. 2
Vc. 2
Cb.
tenuto senza vibr.
ppp

27
sul tasto
poco a poco sul tasto
poco a poco sul tasto
poco a poco sul tasto
poco a poco sul tasto
diminuendo
poco a poco sul tasto
poco a poco sul tasto
poco a poco sul tasto
arm.
ord.
ppp
I Group (A Quarter-tone higher)
II Group
Vn. 1
Vn. 3
Vn. 5
Vn. 7
Vl. 1
Vc. 1
Vn. 2
Vn. 4
Vn. 6
Vl. 2
Vc. 2
Cb.

28
29
I. Group (A Quarter-tone higher)
Vn. 1
Vn. 3
Vn. 5
Vn. 7
Vl. 1
morendo al niente
Vc. 1
II Group
Vn. 2
Vn. 4
Vn. 6
tenuto senza vibr.
Vl. 2
Vc. 2
Cb.

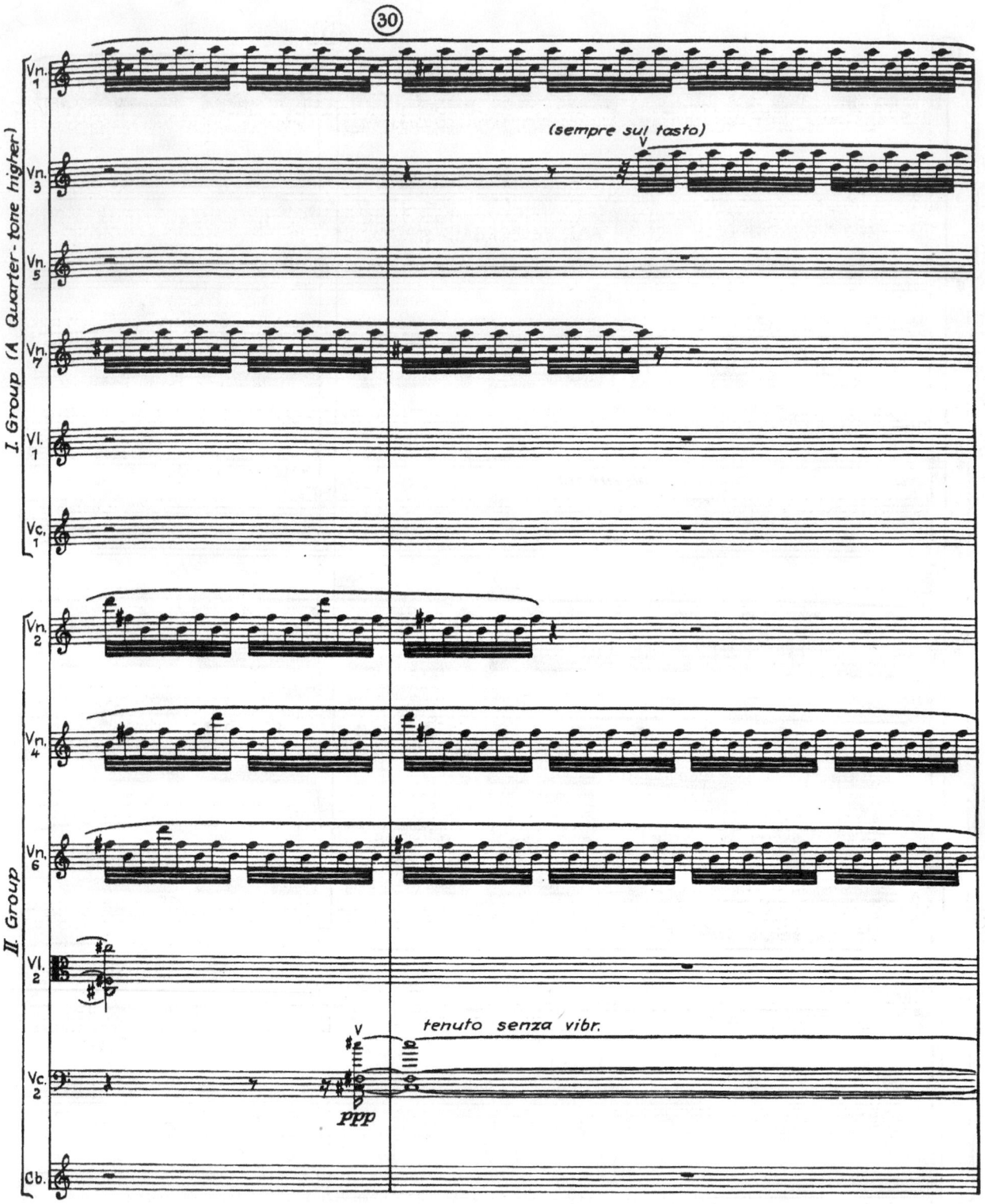
30
I. Group (A Quarter-tone higher)
Vn. 1
Vn. 3
(sempre sul tasto)
Vn. 5
Vn. 7
Vl. 1
Vc. 1
II. Group
Vn. 2
Vn. 4
Vn. 6
Vl. 2
Vc. 2
tenuto senza vibr.
ppp
Cb.

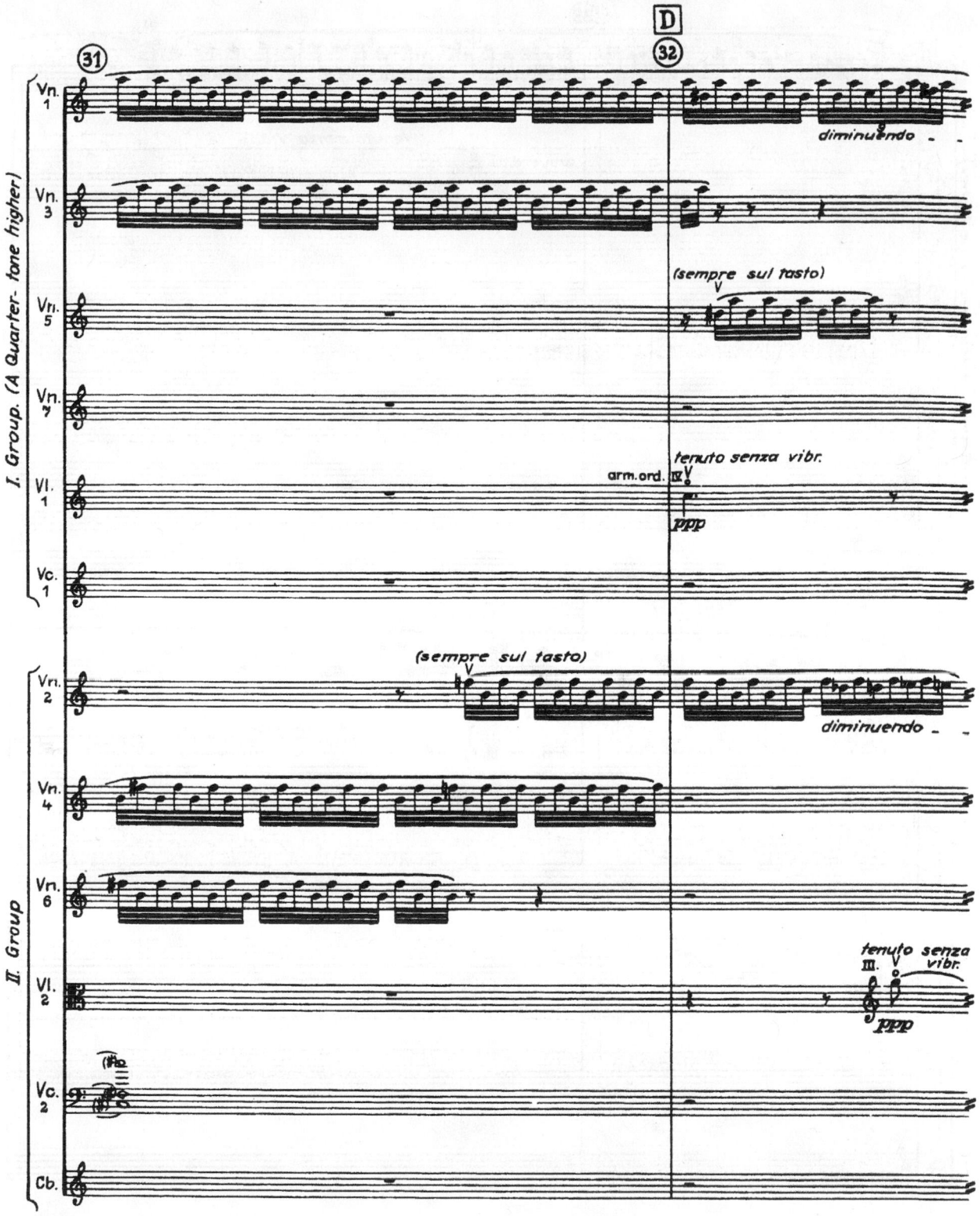
D
31
32
I. Group. (A Quarter- tone higher)
Vn. 1
diminuendo
Vn. 3
Vn. 5
(sempre sul tasto)
Vn. 7
Vl. 1
arm. ord.
tenuto senza vibr.
ppp
Vc. 1
II. Group
Vn. 2
(sempre sul tasto)
diminuendo
Vn. 4
Vn. 6
Vl. 2
tenuto senza vibr.
ppp
Vc. 2
Cb.

*) All the tremoli in this piece: as thick as possible
Alle Tremoli in diesem Stück: so dicht wie möglich

*) All the tremoli in this piece: as thick as possible.
**) Double bass = touch: in the usual (transposed) notation; resulting tone: suono reale.
*) Alle Tremoli in diesem Stück: so dicht wie möglich.
**) Kontrabaß: = Griff: in der üblichen (transponierten) Notierung; resultierender Ton: suono reale.

*) All the tremoli in this piece: as thick as possible.
Alle Tremoli in diesem Stück: so dicht wie möglich.

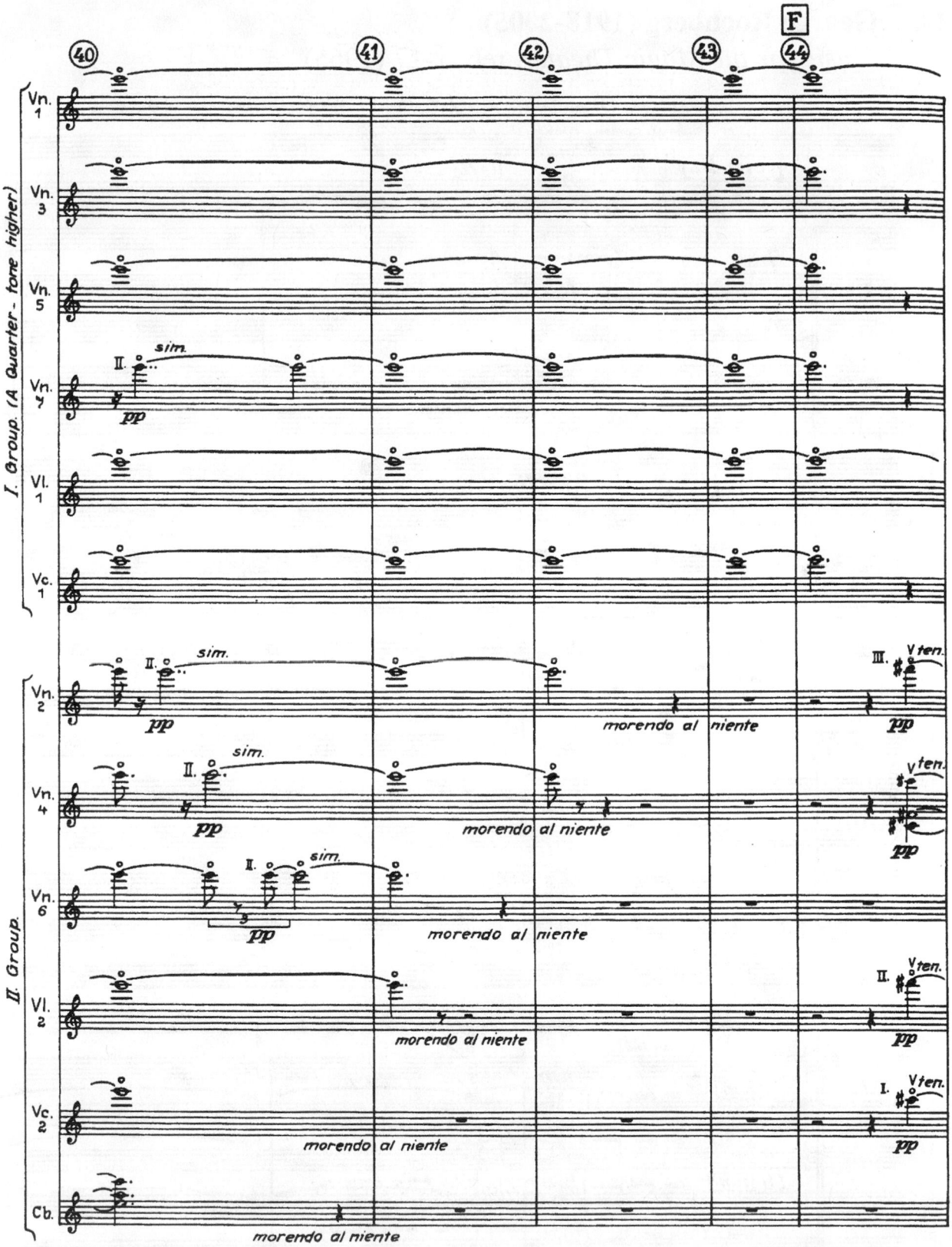
F
40
41
42
43
44
I. Group. (A Quarter-tone higher)
Vn. 1
Vn. 3
Vn. 5
Vn. 7
Vl. 1
Vc. 1
II. Group.
Vn. 2
Vn. 4
Vn. 6
Vl. 2
Vc. 2
Cb.
sim.
pp
morendo al niente
V ten.

33. George Rochberg (1918-2005)

Music for the Magic Theater, reh. 1-17 (1965)

N.B.: All instruments in this score are notated in C.

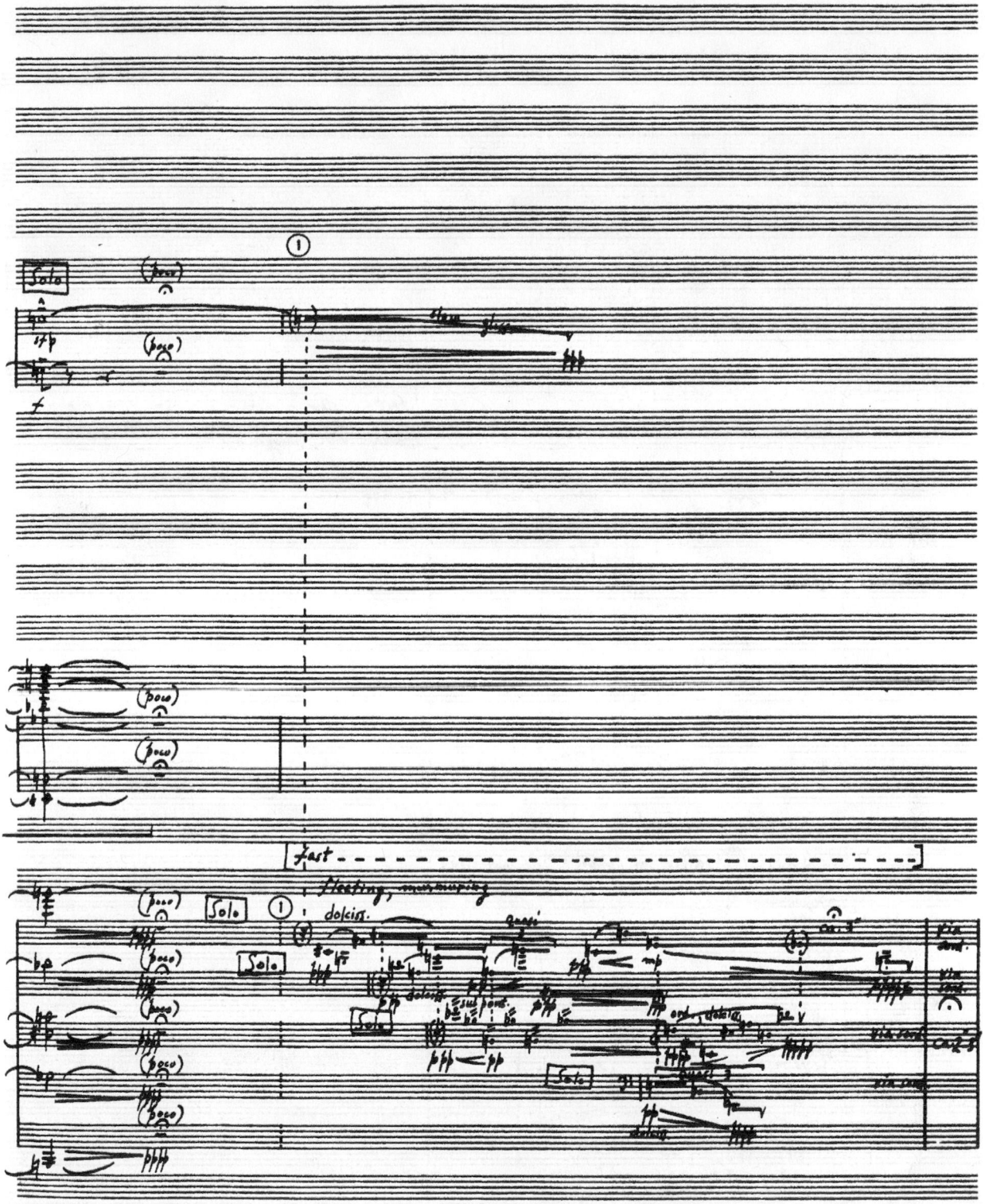
Solo
(poco)
Fast
Fleeting, murmuring
dolcissimo
Solo
quasi
sul ponte
ord.
via sord.

2
fast - - - slow
harmon mute, plunger out
Trpt.
poco
più
Adagio (straffer im Tempo); do not drag
tutti
V.
Va.
C.
B.
sulla corda
sulla corda
2

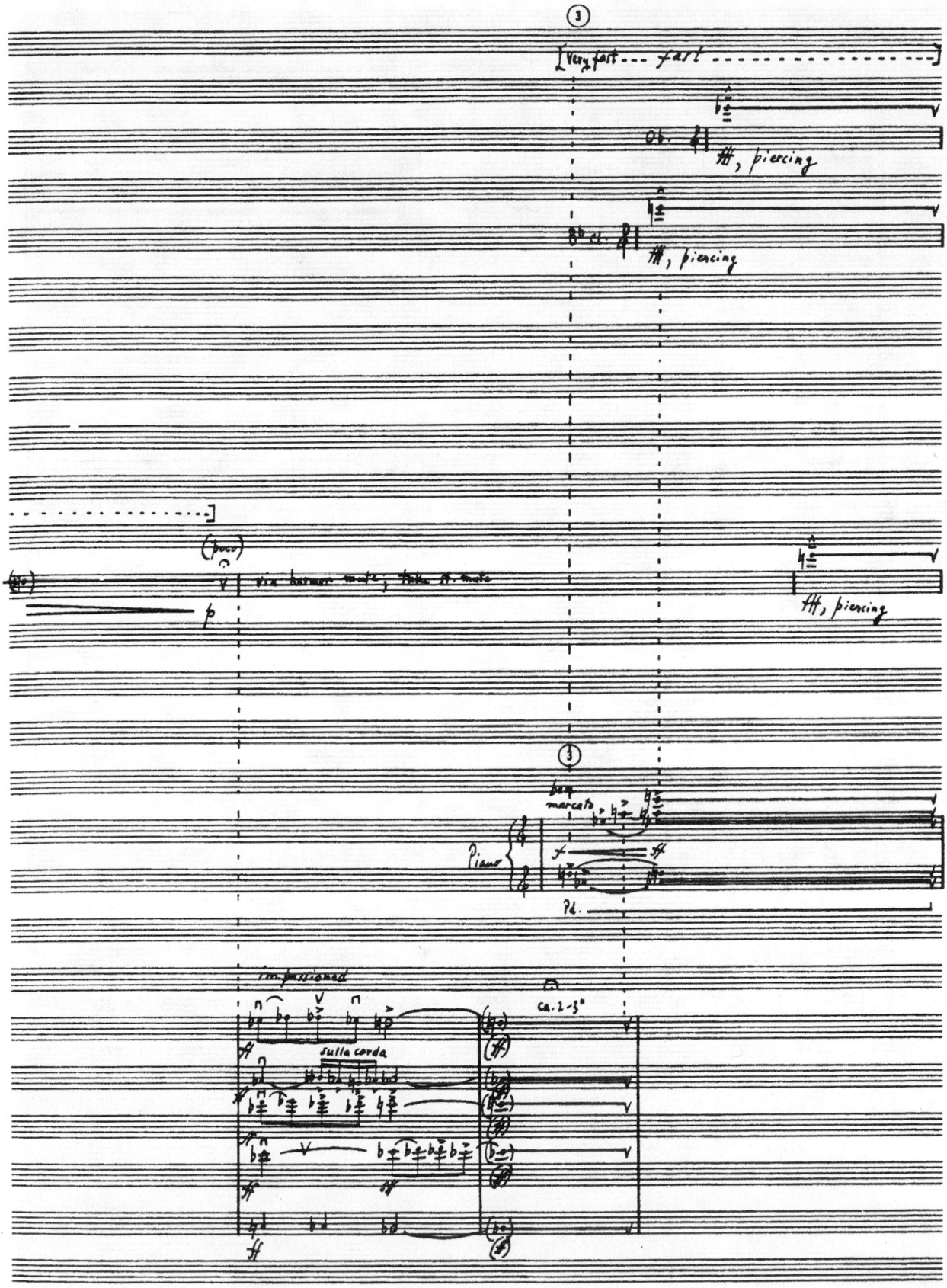
3
[Very fast --- fast
Ob.
ff, piercing
Cl.
ff, piercing
(poco)
via harmon. mute; [illegible] m. mute
p
ff, piercing
3
ben marcato
Piano
Pd.
improvised
ca. 2-3"
sulla corda

Fl. take Picc.
Picc.
Ob.
Cl.
Bn.
a2
Open
Hn.
a2
Open
Trpt.
Trb.
Tba.
Open
Piano
ca. 3-4"

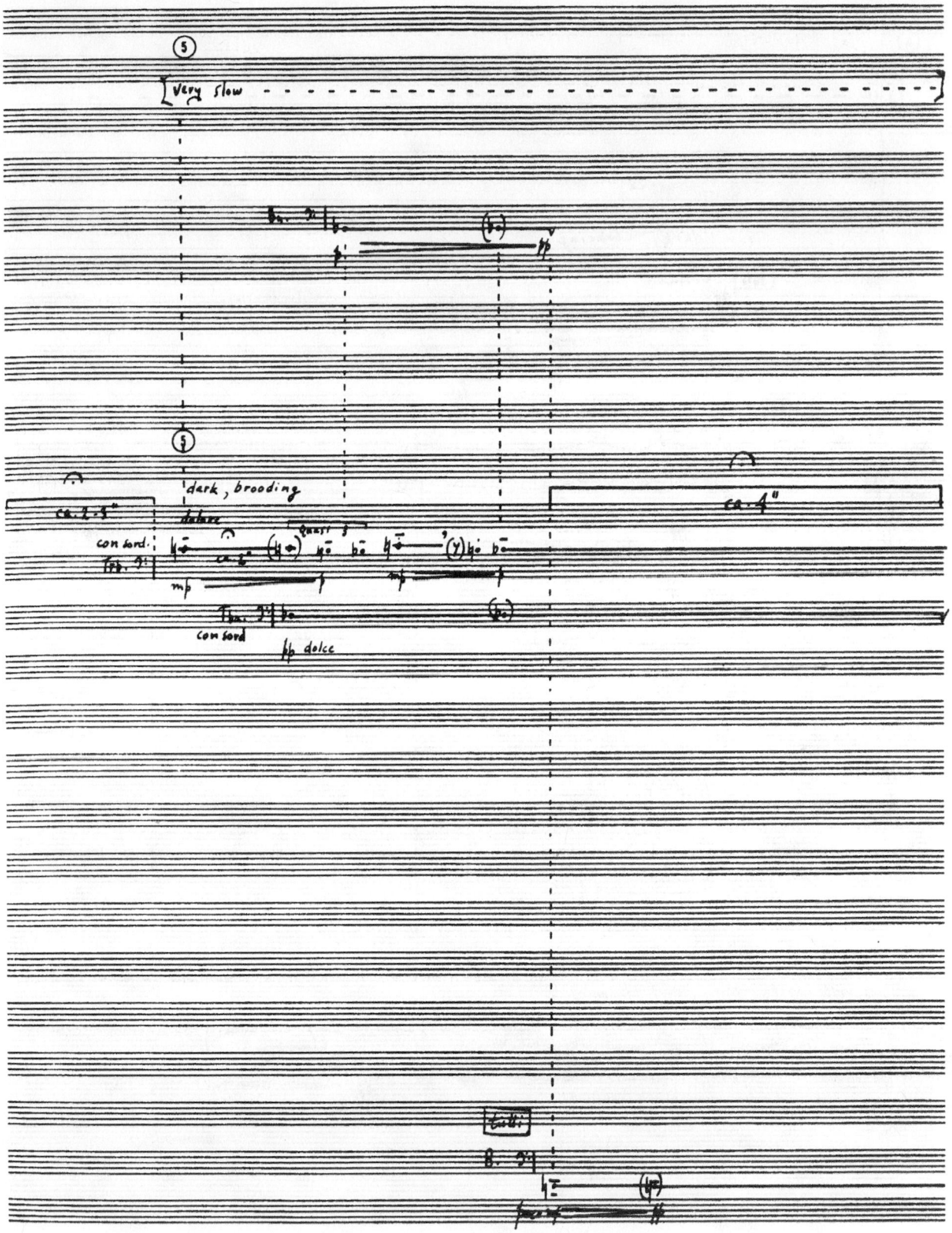
5
Very slow
5
dark, brooding
ca. 2.5"
ca. 4"
con sord.
mp
con sord
pp dolce
Cello
pp

6
Slow
dark, menacing
Solo
(closed)
con sord.
Trb
ca. 3-4"
ca. 2"
6
con molto rubato, wild, dark, brooding
Solo
con sord.
ca. 2"
ca. 2-3"
C
tutti
B
perceptible

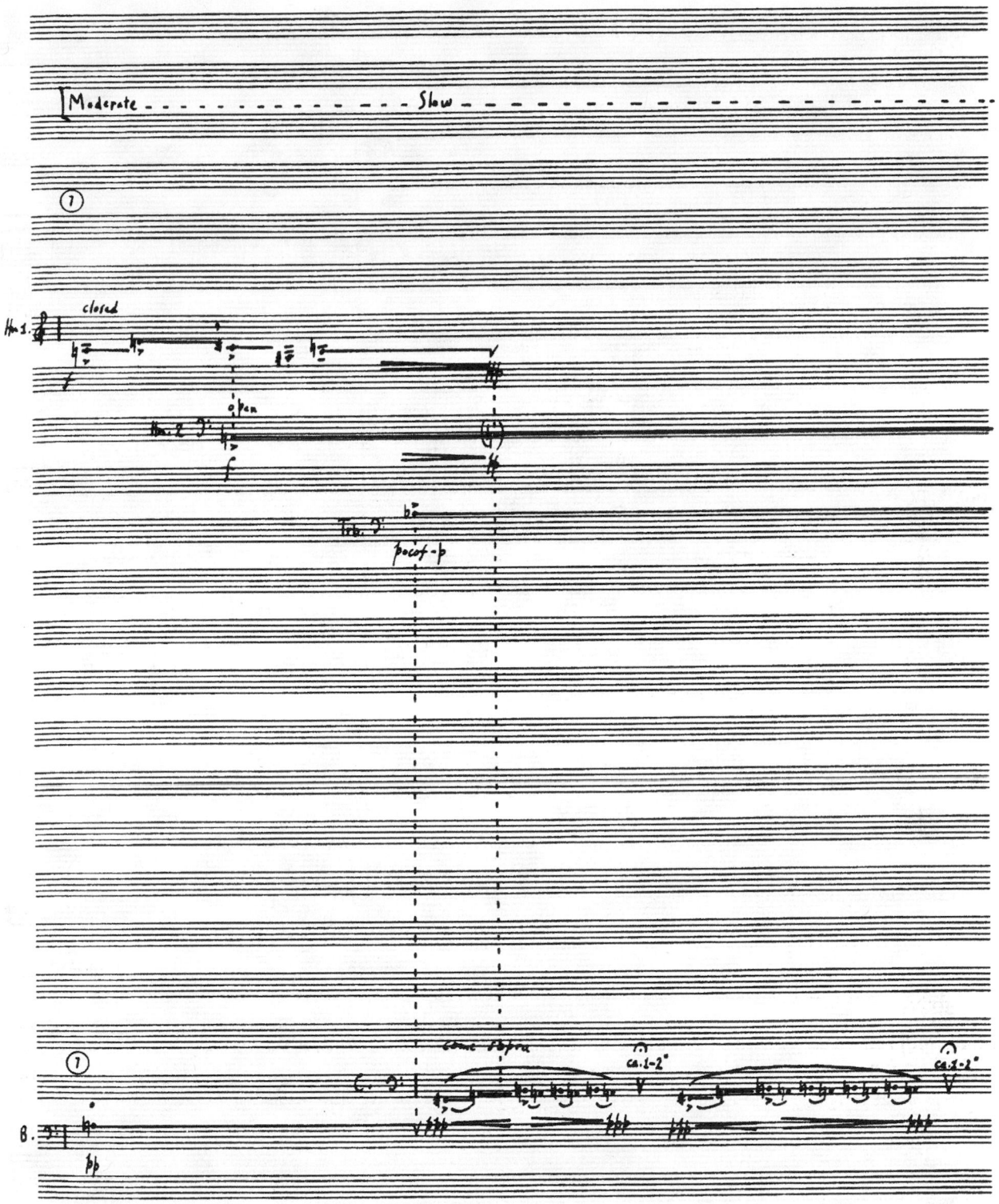
Moderate
Slow
7
closed
Hn. 1.
f
open
Hn. 2
f
Tpt.
poco f - p
7
come sopra
ca. 1-2"
ca. 1-2"
C.
B.
pp

[♩=144-152]
Picc. take Fl.
Fl.
Ob.
Cl.
sff, shrill
sff, shrill
Solo
f ma dolce
Hn. 2
Trpt.
st. mute
open
ff
Trb.
ca. 3"
ff
violent!
Piano
ff
C.
ca. 1-2"
ca. 1-2"
heavily percussive

[♩=72]
Fl.
Ob.
Cl.
Bsn.
Tpt.
Tb.
Piano
distinto
poco Pd.
Tutti
V.
Vc.
C.B.
Pizz. ad.

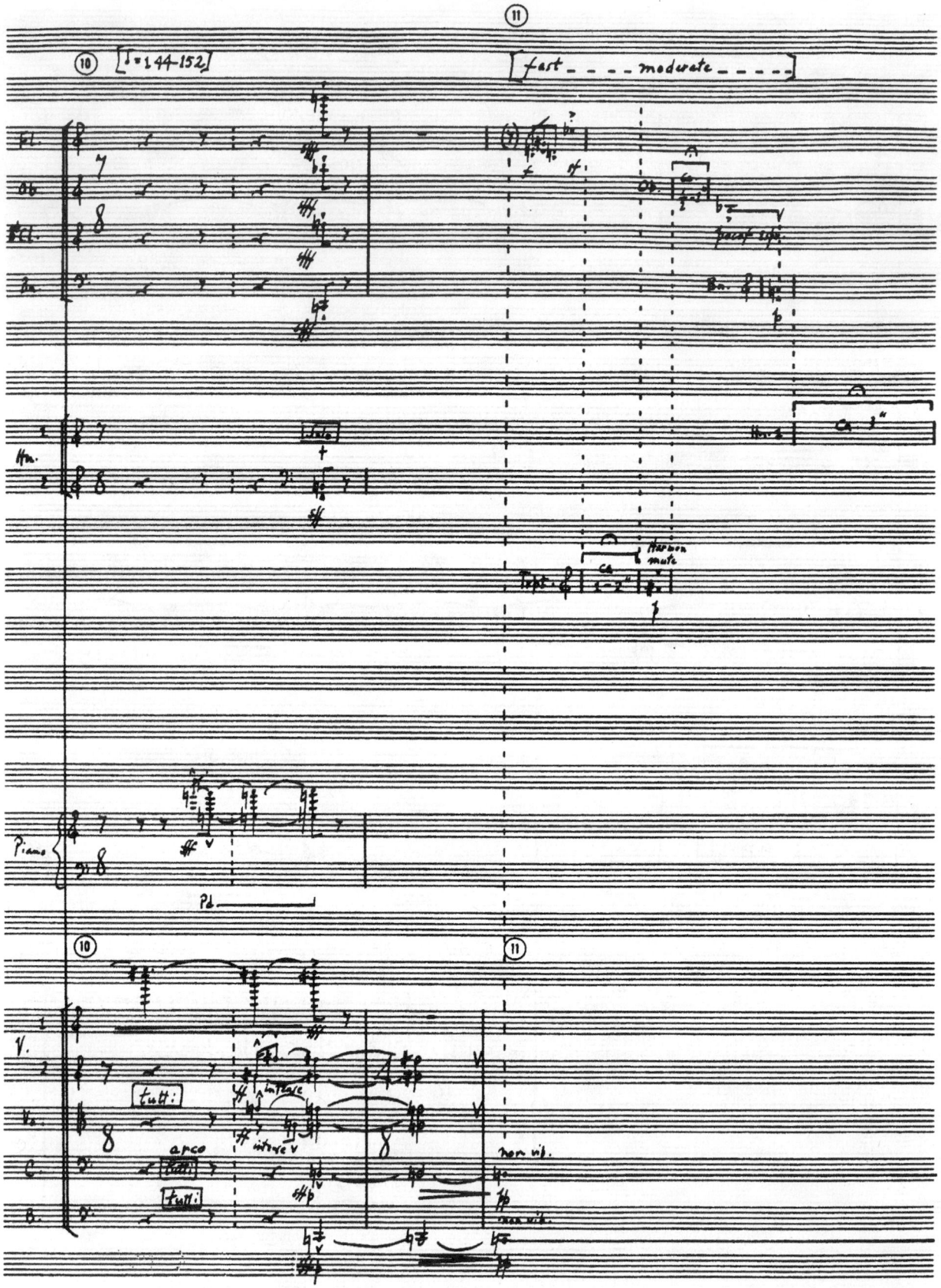
10
♩= 144-152
11
fast - - - - moderate - - - - -
Fl.
Ob.
Cl.
Bn.
Hn.
Trpt.
Harmon mute
Piano
Pd.
V.
tutti
arco
interve
non vib.

Slow
Moderato... very fast... fast to slow
B♭ Cl.
Tacet B♭ Cl.
Hn.
con sord.
senza sord.
Piano
"Allegro"
quasi sul tasto
Mozart String orchestra
V.
Vla.
pp dolcissimo
C.
B.

Fl. take Picc.
B♭ Cl. take E♭ Cl.
13
Solo
open
Hn.
NB. to conductor: set tempo for strings first; then conduct (a piacere) woodwinds and trumpet. It is essential not to synchronize them with the strings.
"Allegro" (♩= 144-152)
13
ca. 2"
V.
Va.
Mozart String orchestra
* 65432

Fl.
Ob.
Cl.
Bn.
Hn.
1
2
Trpt.
V.
1
2
Va.
C.
B.

14
Hn.
1
2
14
V.
1
2
Va.
C.
B.

Moderate - - - - - Very fast
Picc. take Fl.
turbulent
Ob.
15
B♭ Cl. take B♭ Cl.
turbulent
Bn.
Hn.
1
2
push out!
push out!
turbulent
harmon mute
Trpt.
con sord.
dark, menacing
Trb.
con sord.
Tbn.
15
Piano
dex. marcato
p leggiero
ff (hard)
sff
sff
Pd.
V.
1
2
Va.
C.
B.
NB. Build passage (through p. 19) around antiphony of Horns 2 and Trb./Tuba. Press tempo hard. Mood is menacing, turbulent.

turbulent
16
[as fast as possible]
Fl.
Ob.
turbulent
B♭ Cl.
Bn.
42
dark, menacing
Hn.
poco f
dark, menacing
poco f
Tpt.
16
Trb.
Tba.
poco f
poco f
Piano
senza pedale

ca. 3"
fff, shrill, piercing!
fff, shrill, piercing!
fff, piercing!
fff, piercing!
17
poco f-pp
push out!
ca. 3"
sfp
sf
push out!
poco f-pp
fff, piercing!
push out!
ca. 5"
poco sfp
sf
sfp
poco sfp
sf
sfp
push out!
Tutti
non vib.
* Cluster: divisi
17

34. Luciano Berio (1925-2003)

Sinfonia, III ("In ruhig fliessender Bewegung"), mm. 1-120 (to reh. F) (1968)

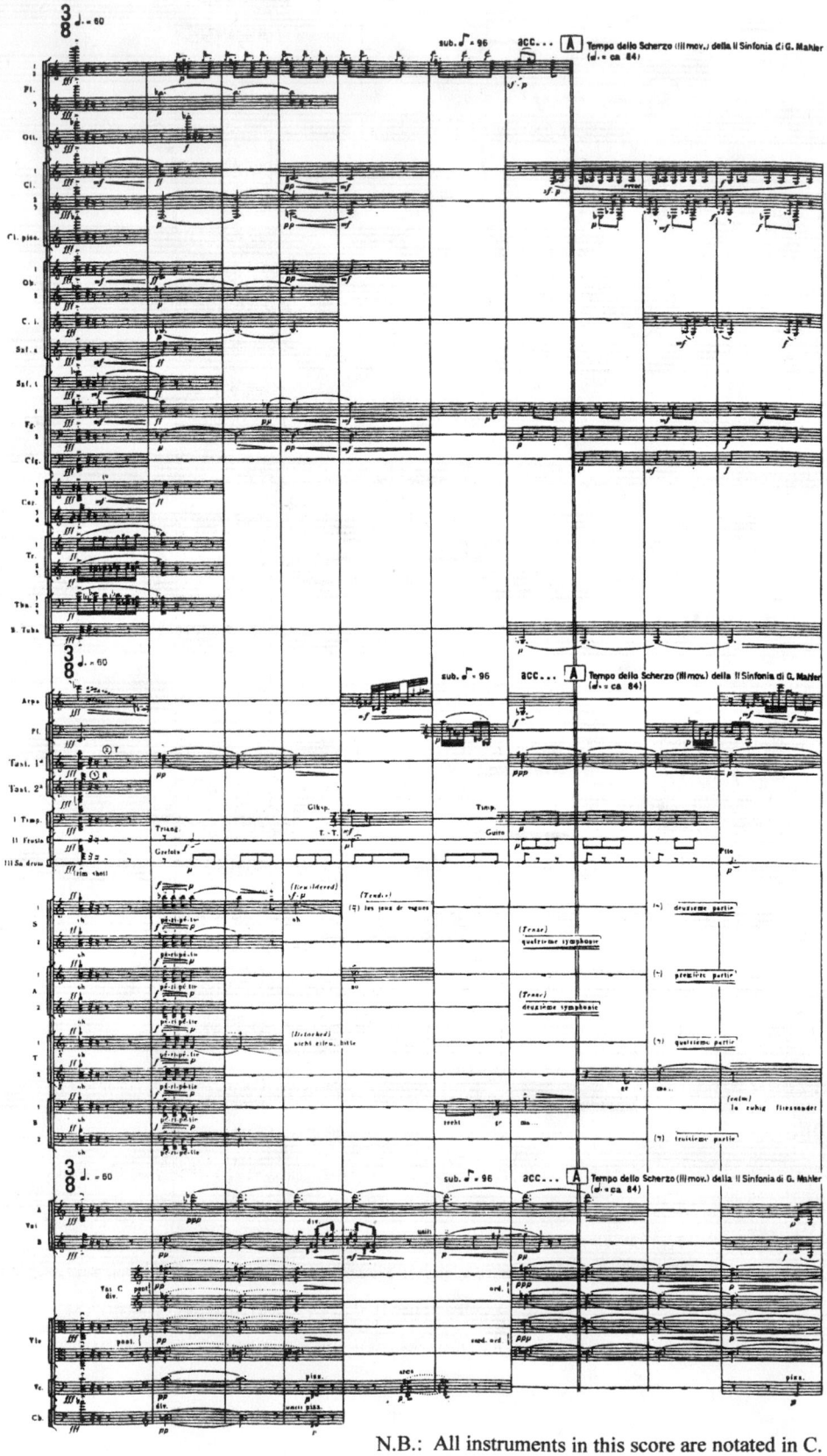

N.B.: All instruments in this score are notated in C.

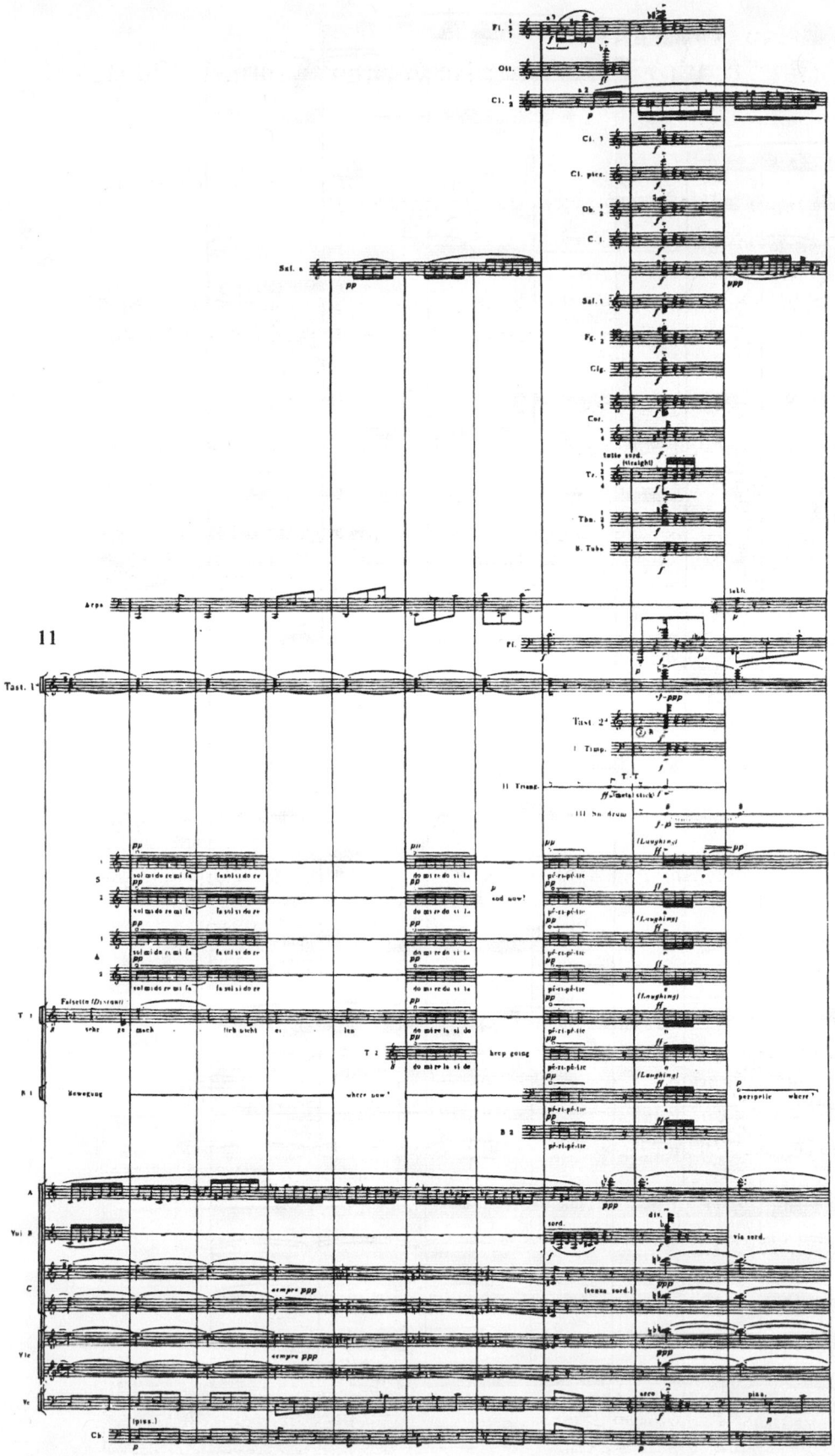
Fl. 1 2 3
Ott.
Cl. 1 2
Cl. 3
Cl. pice.
Ob. 1 2
C. i.
Sal. s.
Sal. t.
Fg. 1 2
Clg.
Cor. 1 3 4
Tr. 1 2 3 4
Tbn. 1 2 3
B. Tuba
Arpa
11
Pf.
Tast. 1
Tast. 2
I Timp.
II Timp.
III Sn. drum
S 1
S 2
A 1
A 2
Falsetto (Disraeli)
T 1
T 2
B 1
B 2
Bewegung
where now?
perspirie where?
Vni I
Vni II
C
Vla
Vc
Cb
sempre ppp
(senza sord.)
via sord.
(piss.)

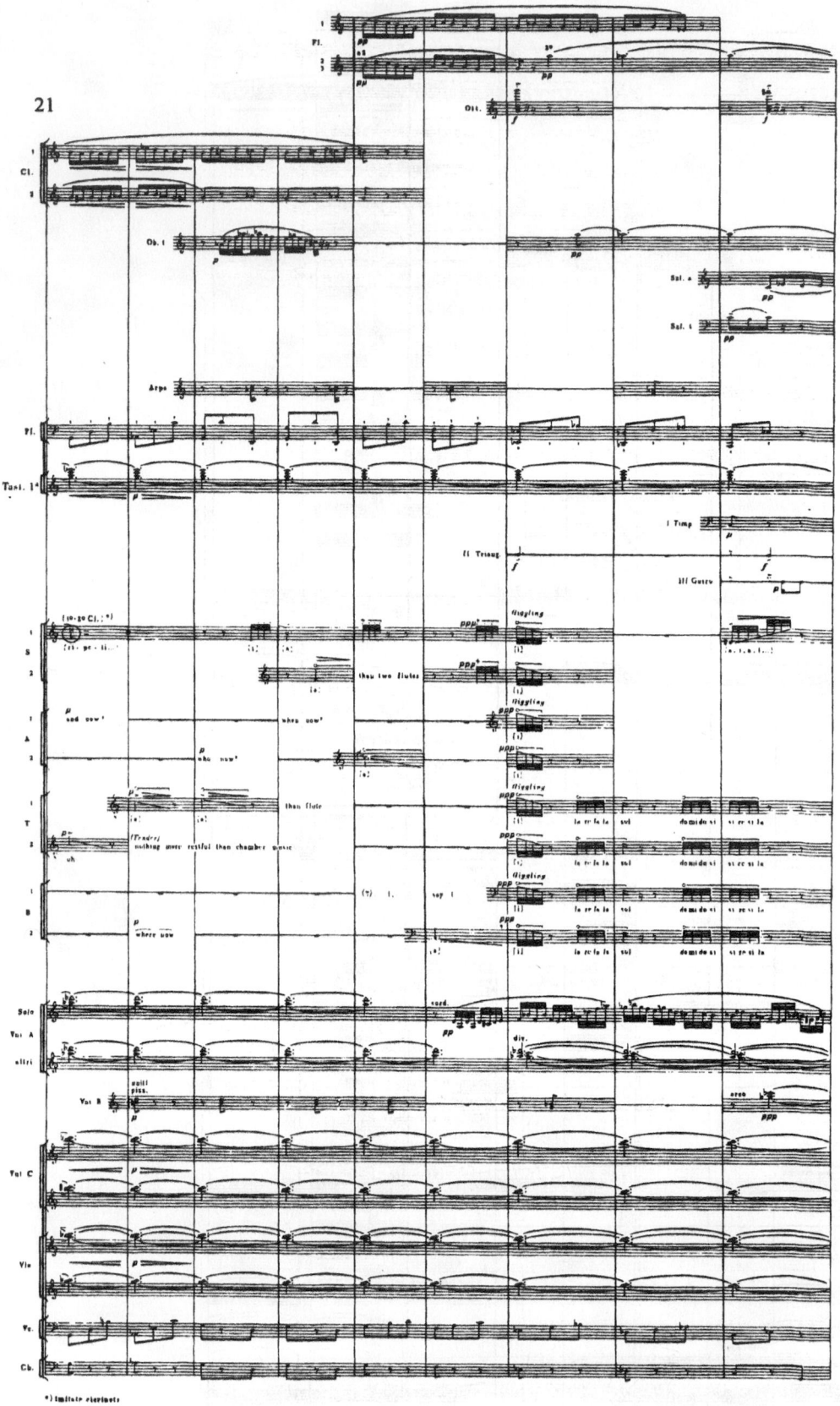

*) imitate clarinets

*) "Tooth-tremolo"

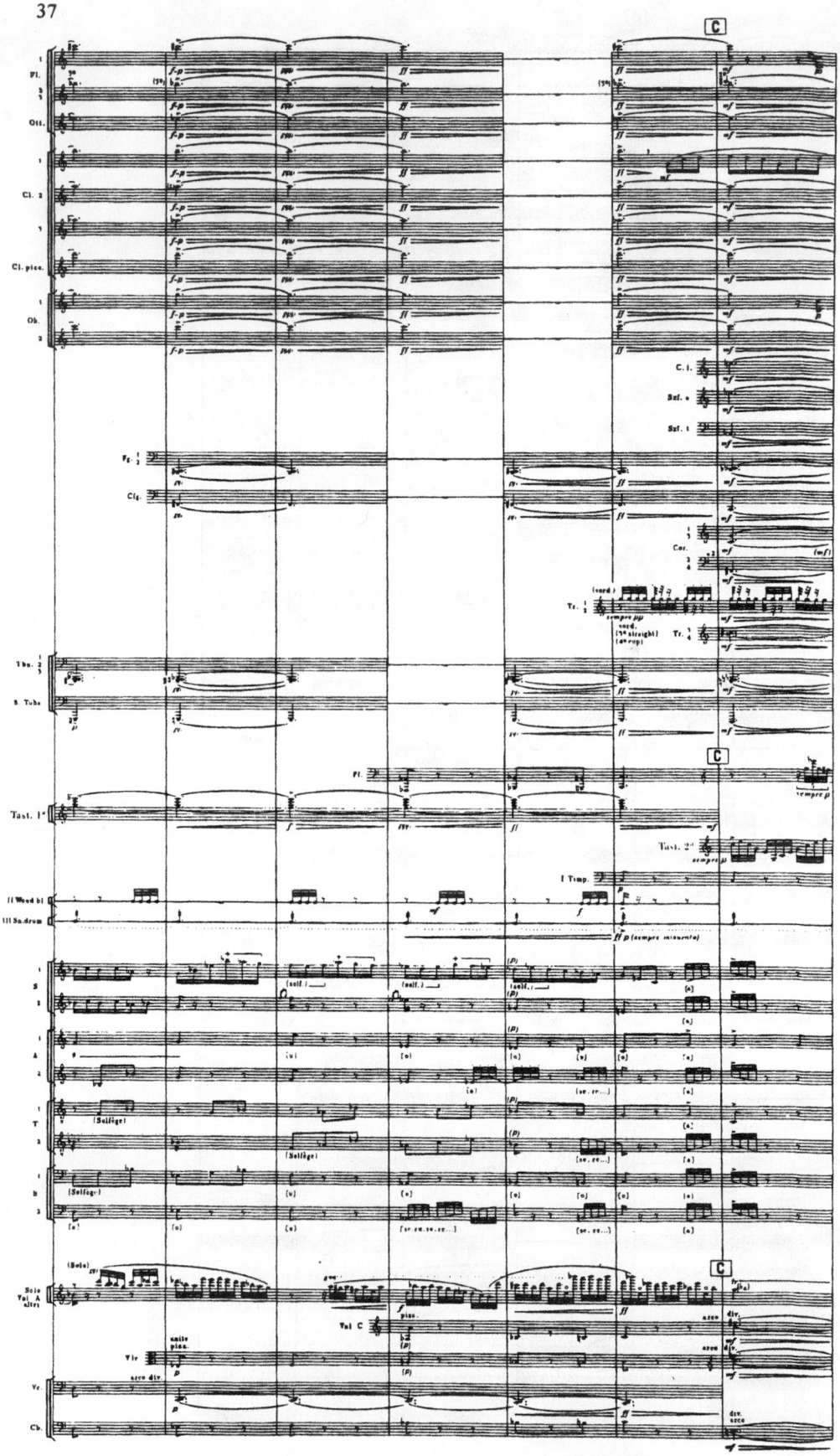
C
Fl.
Ott.
Cl. 2
Cl. pice.
Ob.
C. i.
Sax. a
Sax. t
Fg. 1
Clg.
Cor.
Tr.
Tbn.
B. Tbn.
Tast. 1°
Tast. 2°
I Timp.
II Wood bl
III Sn.drum
S
A
T
B
Solo
Val. A
altri
Val. C
Vln
Vc.
Cb.
(Solfège)
(solf.)
(se. re...)
(se. re. se. re...)
(Solo)
unis
pizz.
arco div.
div.
arco

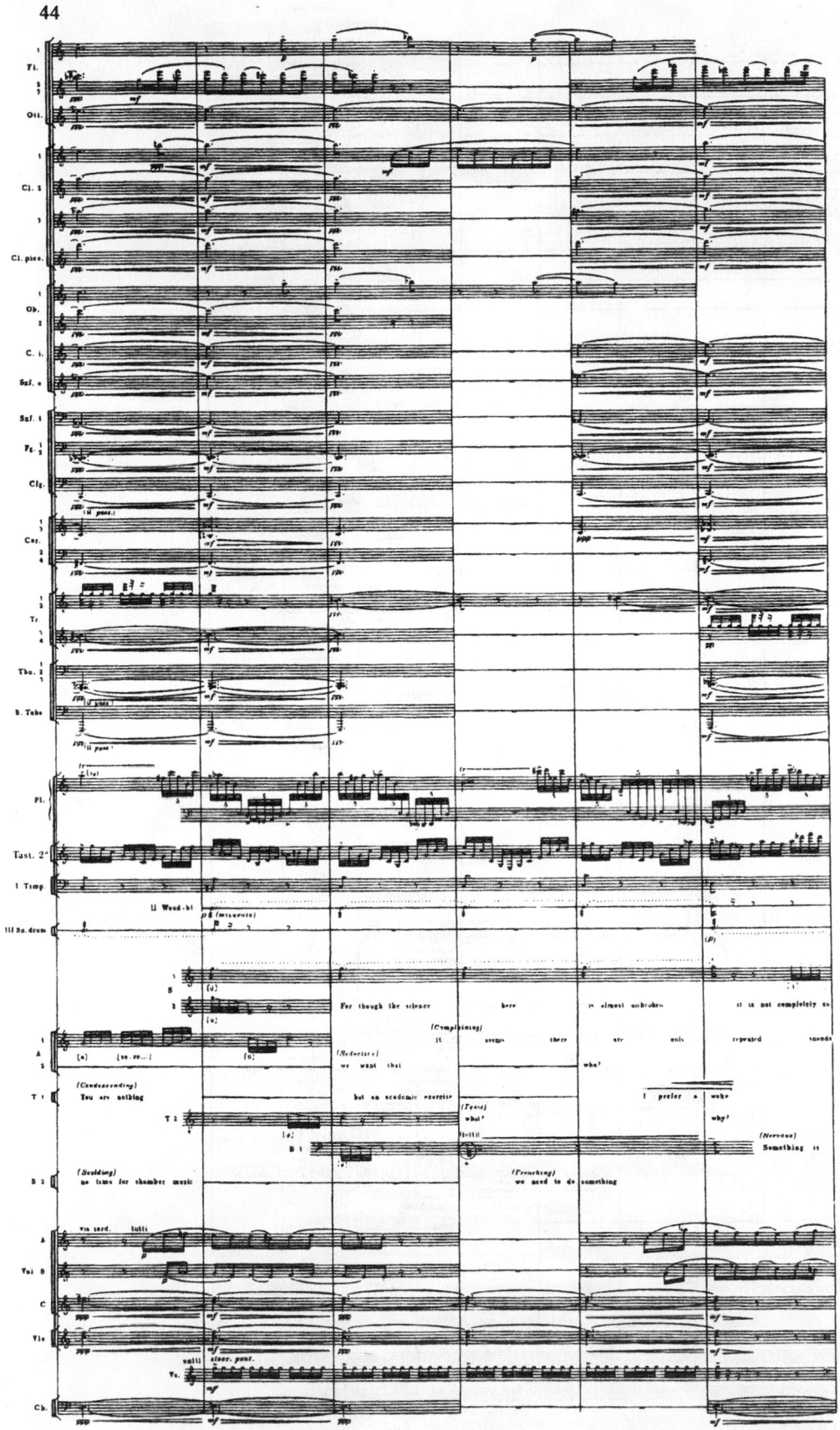
44
Fl.
Ott.
Cl. 1
Cl. piccc.
Ob.
C. i.
Sxf. a
Sxf. t
Fg.
Clg.
Cor.
Tr.
Tbn. 2
B. Tuba
Pl.
Tast. 2°
I Timp.
III Sn. drum
S
A
T 1
T 2
B 1
B 2
Vni B
C
Vla
Vc.
Cb.
For though the silence here is almost unbroken it is not completely so
(Complaining) it seems there are only repeated sounds
(Nedantic) we want that
who?
(Condescending) You are nothing
but an academic exercise
I prefer a wake
(Tense) what?
why?
(Nervous) Something is
(Scolding) no time for chamber music
(Preaching) we need to do something
vin sord. tutti
tutti

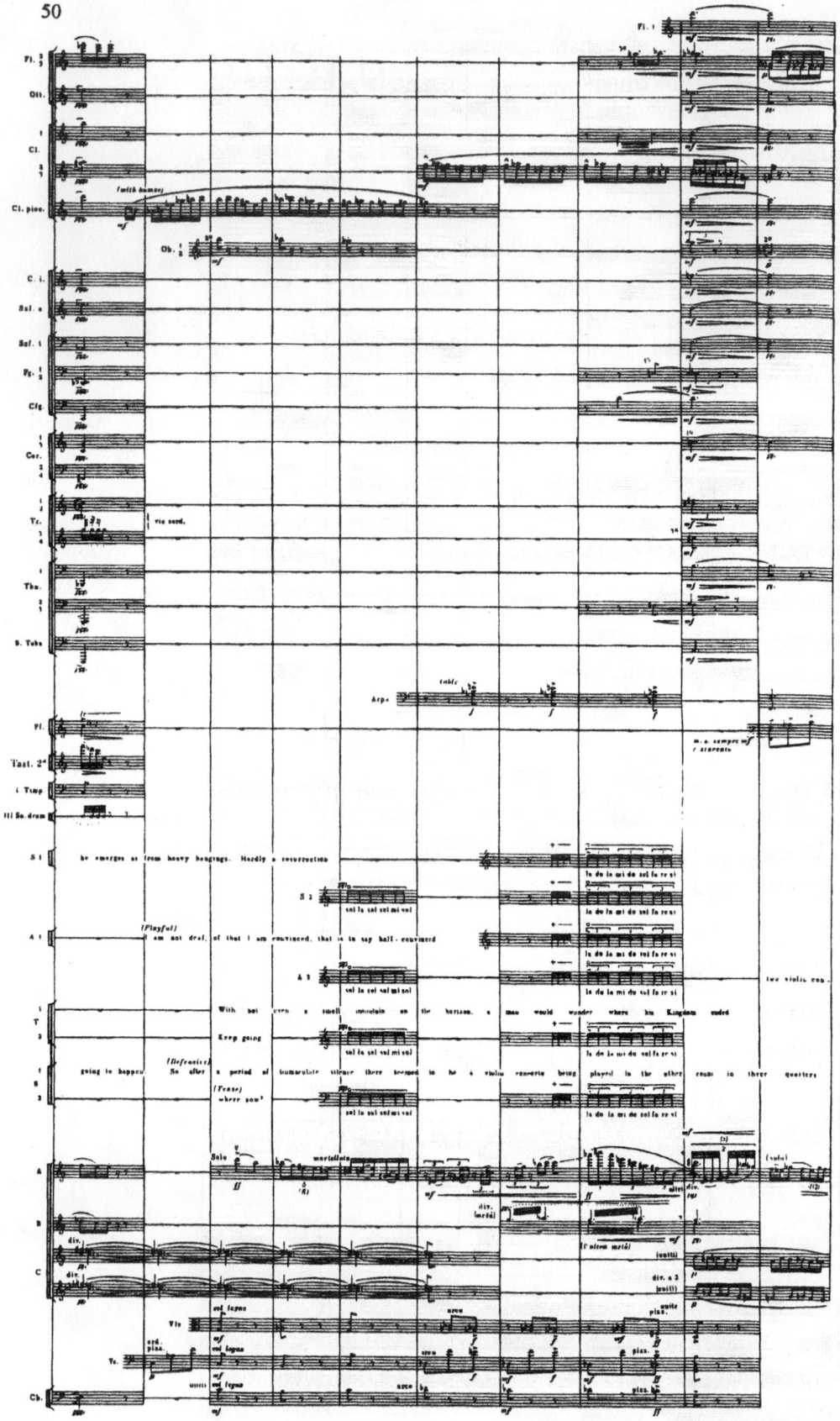
Fl. 1
Ott.
Cl.
Cl. piccc.
(with humor)
Ob. 1
C. i.
Sax. a
Sax. t
Fg. 1
Clg.
Cor.
Tr.
vio sord.
Tbn.
B. Tuba
Arpa
table
Fl.
Tast. 2ª
i Timp.
iii Sn. drum
S 1
he emerges as from heavy hangings. Hardly a resurrection
S 2
A 1
(Playful)
I am not deaf, of that I am convinced, that is to say half-convinced
A 2
two violin con.
T
With not even a small mountain on the horizon, a man would wonder where his kingdom ended
Keep going
B
going to happen
(Hesitant)
So after a period of humorous silence there seemed to be a violin concerto being played in the other room in three quarters
(Tease)
where now?
Solo
martellato
div.
(solo)
(unis)
div. a 3
(unis)
arco
pizz.
Vle
Vc.
Cb.

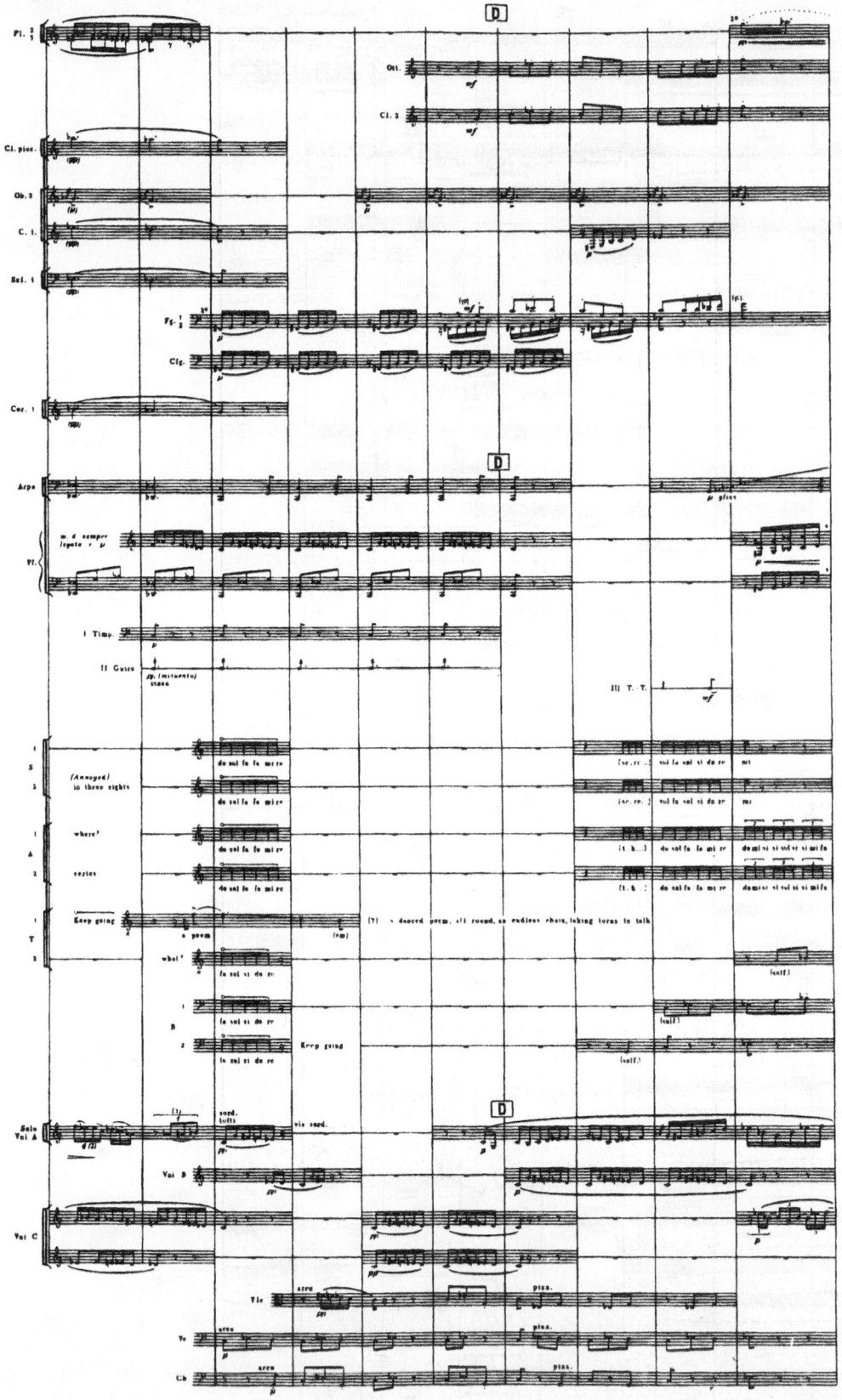
D
Fl. 1 2
Ob.
Cl. 2
Cl. picc.
Ob. 2
C. I.
Bcl. 1
Fg. 1 2
Clg.
Cor. 1
Arpe
m. d. sempre legato
Pf.
I Timp.
II Guiro
III T. T.
(Annoyed) in three eights
where?
easier
Keep going
a poem
what?
Keep going
Solo Vcl A
Vcl B
Vcl C
Vle
Vc
Cb
arco
pizz.

Fl.
Ott.
Cl.
Cl. 1
Ob.
C. i.
Sal. s
Sal. t
Fg.
Clg.
Cor.
Tr.
sord. (straight)
trunk sord.
Tbn.
B. Tuba
Arpa
Pf.
II Su. drum
(metal stick)
III T. T.
S
(soll.)
Keep going
A
(soll.)
T
(soll.)
(Defensive)
This represents at least
B
A
div.
Vcl. B
C
Vla
arco
pizz.
Vc.
Cb.

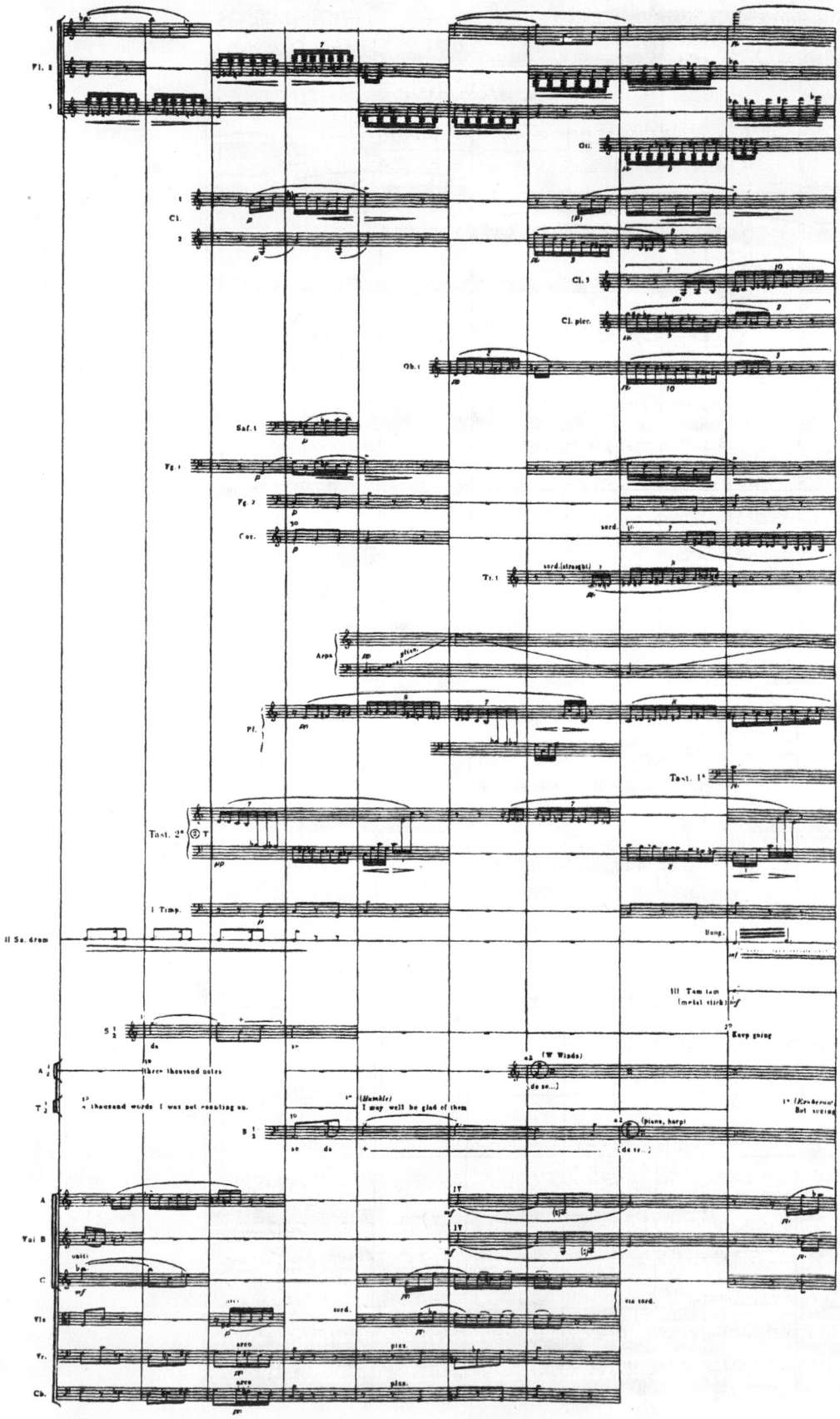
Fl. 1
Ott.
Cl.
Cl. 3
Cl. picc.
Ob. 1
Saf. 1
Fg. 1
Fg. 2
Cor.
sord.
Tr. 1
sord. (straight)
Arpa
Pf.
Tast. 1°
Tast. 2°
I Timp.
II Sn. drum
Bong.
III Tam tam
(metal stick)
Keep going
A
T
B
(W Winds)
(Humble)
I may well be glad of them
(piano, harp)
Vol B
Vla
Vc.
Cb.
sord.
via sord.
arco
pizz.

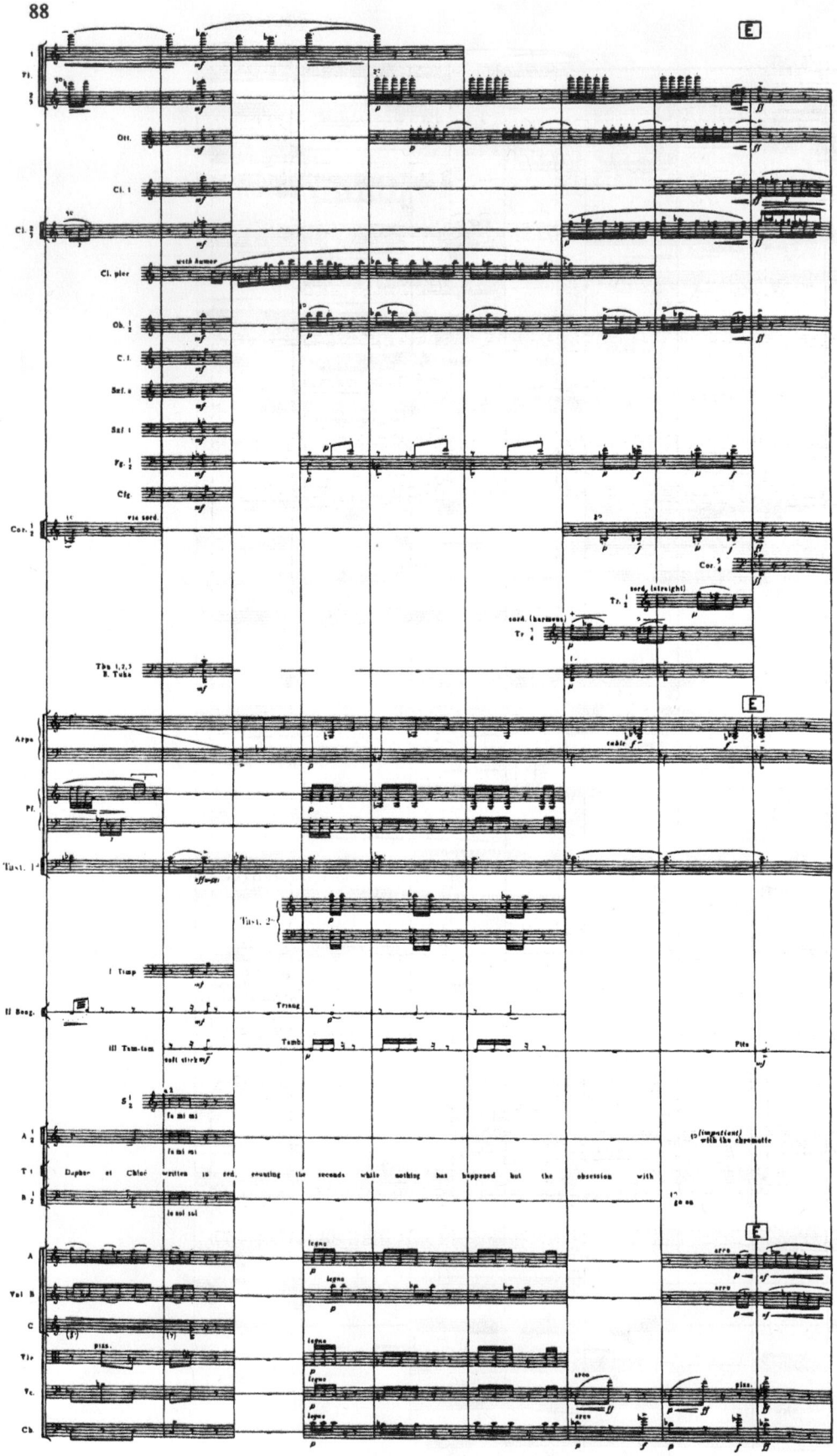
E
Fl.
Ott.
Cl. 1
Cl. 2/3
with humor
Cl. pier
Ob. 1/2
C. I.
Sax. a
Sax. t
Fg. 1/2
Cfg.
via sord.
Cor. 1/2
Cor. 3/4
sord. (straight)
Tr. 1/2
sord. (harmon)
Tr. 3/4
Tbn. 1,2,3
B. Tuba
Arpa
cadz
Pf.
Tast. 1
Tast. 2
I Timp
II Bong.
Triang
III Tam-tam
Tamb.
soft stick
Flto
S 1/2
fa mi mi
A 1/2
fa mi mi
(impatient)
with the chromatic
T 1
Daphnis et Chloé written in red, counting the seconds while nothing has happened but the obsession with
B 1/2
la sol sol
go on
A
legno
arco
Vol. B
C
pizz.
Vla.
Vc.
Cb

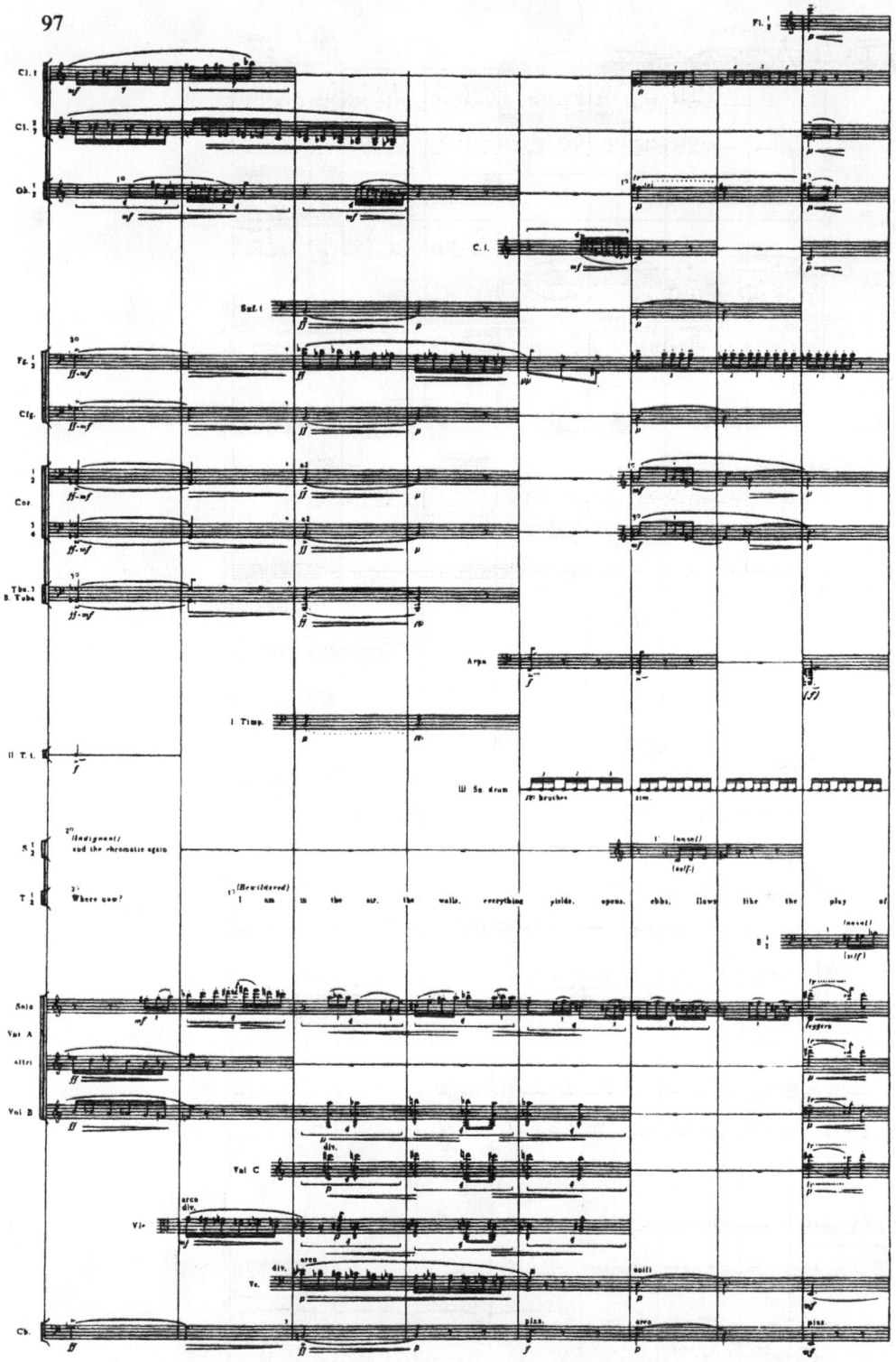
97
Fl. 1/2
Cl. 1
Cl. 2/3
Ob. 1/2
C. I.
Saxf. I
Fg. 1/2
Clfg.
Cor.
Tbn. 3
B. Tuba
Arpa
I Timp.
II T. I.
III Sn drum
S. 1/2
(Indignant)
and the chromatic again
T. 1/2
Where now?
(Bewildered)
I am in the air, the walls, everything yields, opens, ebbs, flows like the play of
B. 1/2
Solo
Vln A
altri
Vln B
div.
Vln C
arco
div.
Vla
div.
arco
Vc.
Cb.
pizz.
arco
pizz.

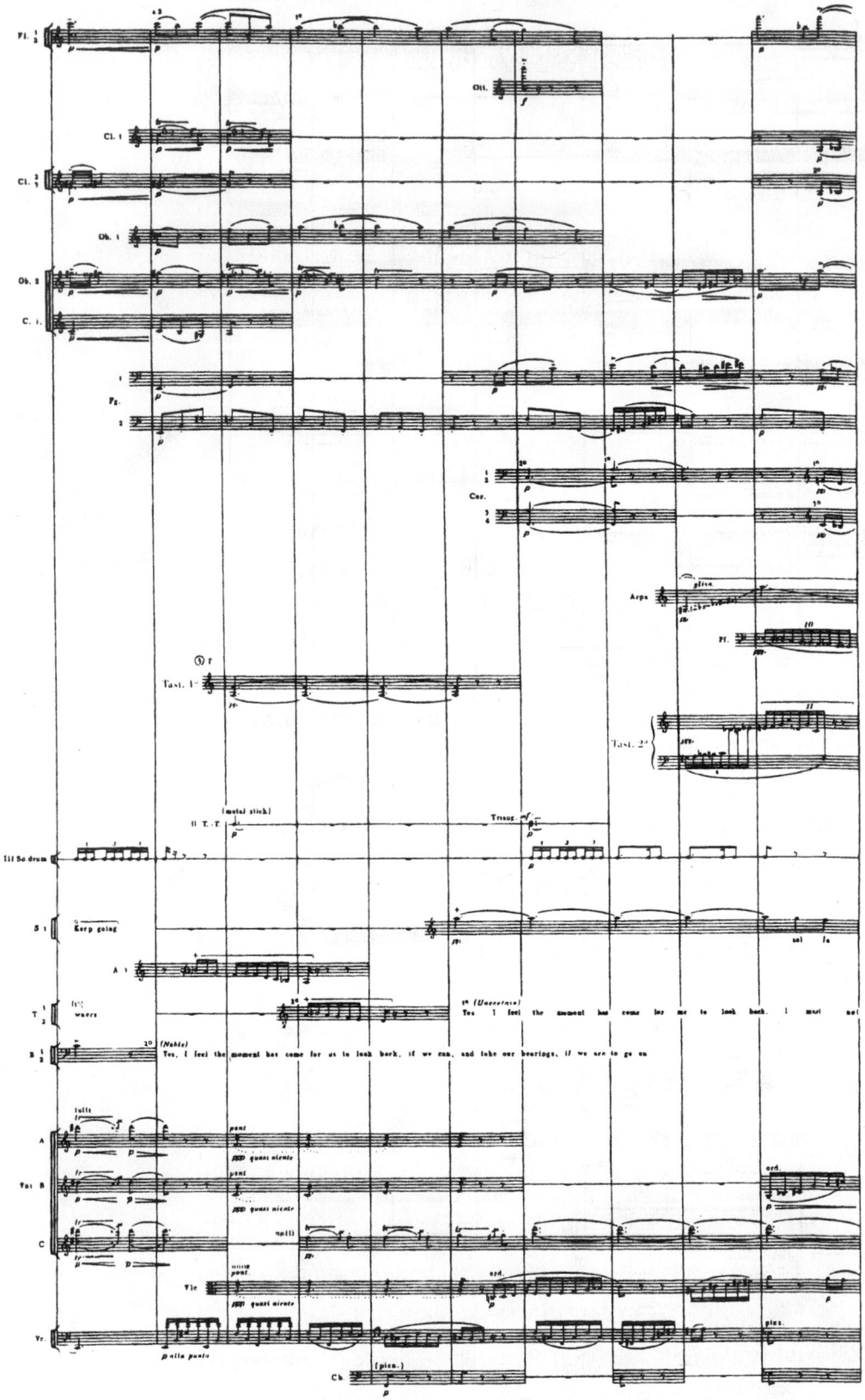
Fl. 1 2
Ott.
Cl. 1
Cl. 2 3
Ob. 1
Ob. 2
C. i.
Fg.
Cor.
Arpa
glice.
Pf.
Tast. 1°
Tast. 2°
(metal) stick)
Triang.
lil So drum
S 1
Keep going
sul fa
A 1
T 1 2
waves
1° (Uncertain)
Yes I feel the moment has come for me to look back. I must sul
B 1 2
2° (Noble)
Yes, I feel the moment has come for us to look back, if we can, and take our bearings, if we are to go on
tutti
A
Vni B
C
punt
quasi niente
sulli
ord.
Vle
Vc.
p alla punta
Cb
(pizz.)

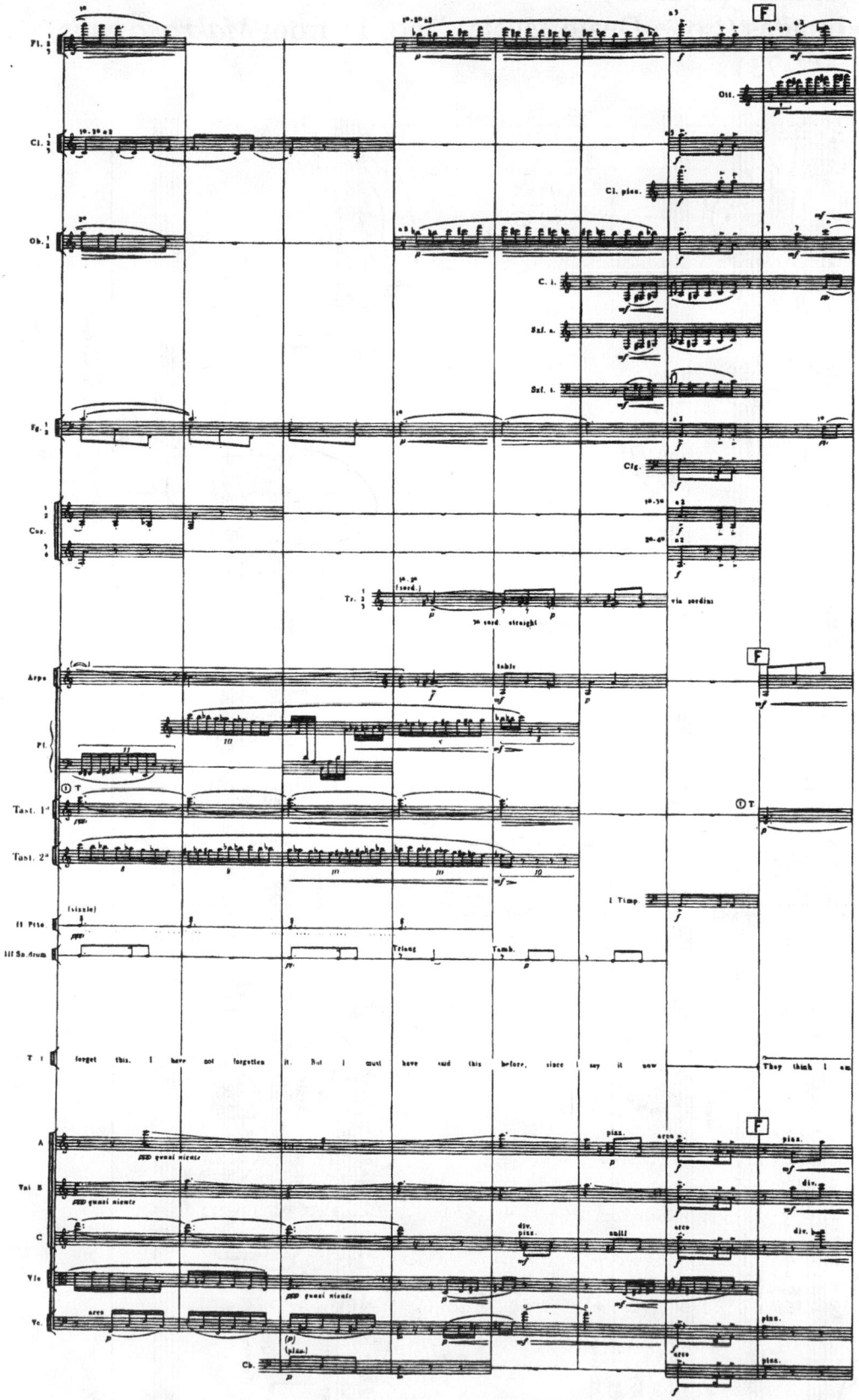
Fl.
Ott.
Cl.
Cl. pico.
Ob.
C. i.
Sax. s.
Sax. t.
Fg.
Clg.
Cor.
Tr.
via sordini
Arpa
table
Pl.
Tast. 1°
Tast. 2°
I Timp.
II Pito
III Sn.drum
Triang.
Tamb.
T
forget this. I have not forgotten it. But I must have said this before, since I say it now
They think I am
A
pizz.
arco
Vai B
div.
C
div. pizz.
unis.
Vle
Vc.
Cb.

35. George Crumb (b. 1923)

"Dream Images (Love-Death Music)," no. 11 from *Makrokosmos*, vol. 1 (1972-73)

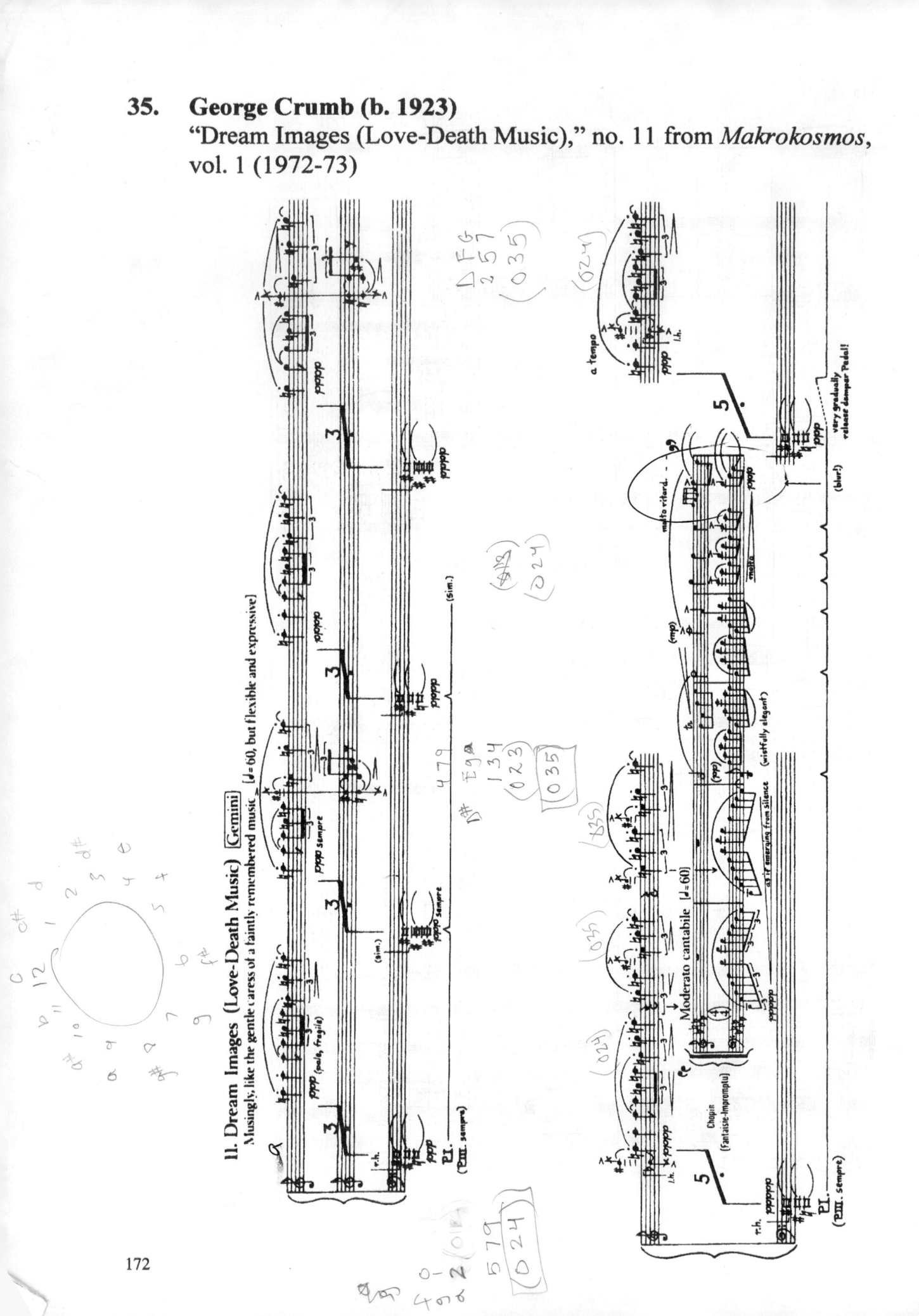

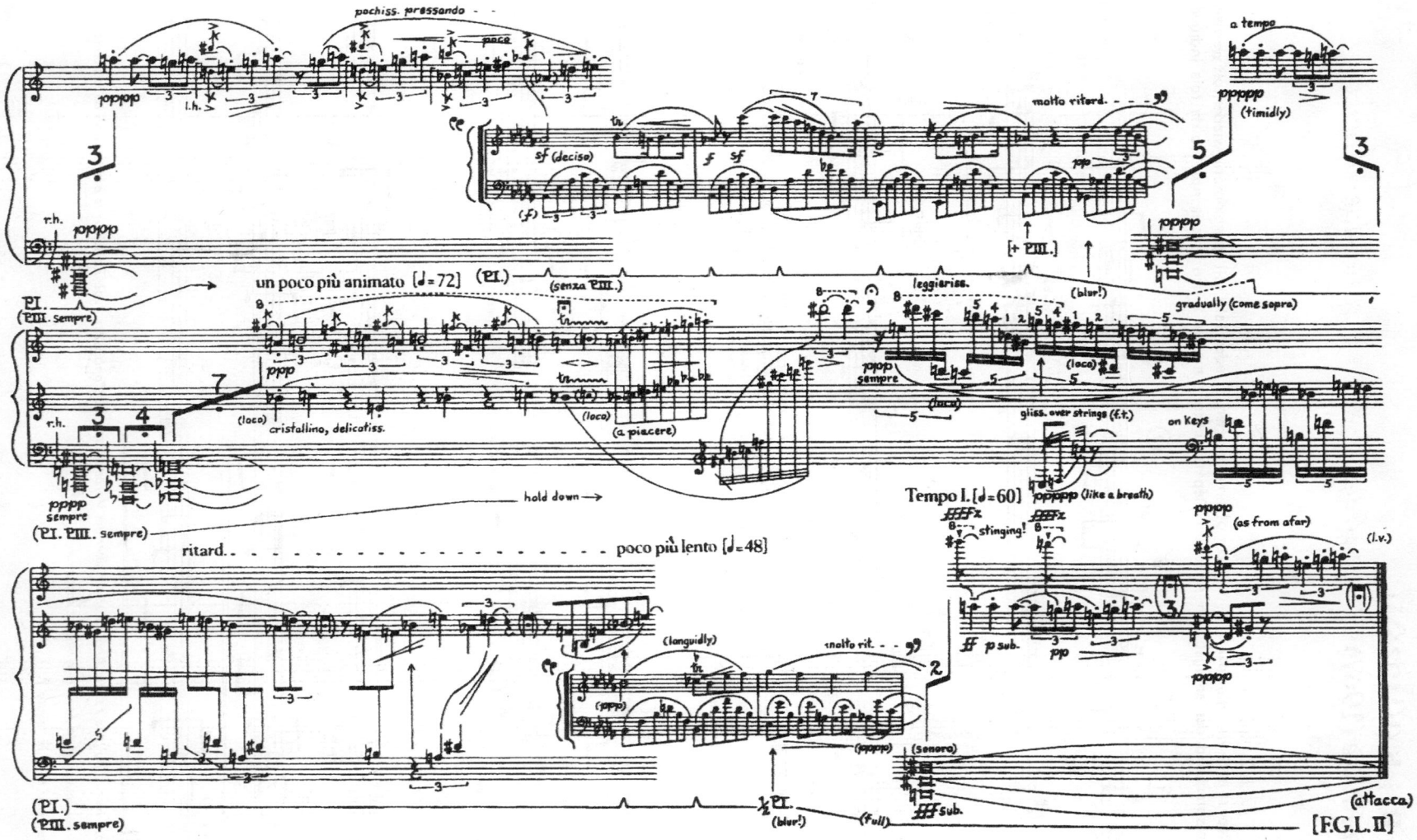
pochiss. pressando
pace
l.h.
r.h.
sf (deciso)
molto ritard.
a tempo
(timidly)
[+ PIII.]
un poco più animato [♩=72]
(PI.)
(senza PIII.)
(PI. PIII. sempre)
leggierissimo
(blur!)
gradually (come sopra)
(loco)
cristallino, delicatiss.
(a piacere)
gliss. over strings (f.t.)
on keys
(like a breath)
hold down
Tempo I. [♩=60]
stinging!
(as from afar)
(l.v.)
ritard.
poco più lento [♩=48]
(languidly)
molto rit.
(senza)
(senora)
(attacca)
[F.G.L.II]

36. Steve Reich (b. 1936)
Violin Phase (1967)

♩ = ca. 144

Repeat each bar approximately number of times written. / Jeder Takt soll approximativ wiederholt werden entsprechend der angegebenen Anzahl. / Répétez chaque mesure à peu près le nombre de fois indiqué

1) *see notes for pre-recording tape / siehe Anmerkungen über die Vorbereitung des Tonbandes / voir notes sur la préparation de la bande*

2) *sehr geringfügiges accelerando / très légèrement accelerando*

3) *tempo 1 fortsetzen / tenir le tempo 1*

9
9a
TAPE TRK. 2 (VIOLIN 1)
TAPE TRK. 2 (VIOLIN 3)
Result of TAPE TRACK 2 (VIOLINS 1+3)
(x4 - 6)
(x4 - 6)
VIOLIN (VIOLIN 2)
Fade in
f
Alternate Resulting Pattern (see notes)
9b
10
(x4 6)
(x4 - 6)
Fade out
Fade in
10a
10b
TAPE TRK. 2 (VIOLIN 1)
APE TRK. 2 (VIOLIN 3)
Result of TAPE TRK. 2 (VIOLINS 1+3)
(x4 6)
(x4 - 6)
VIOLIN (VIOLIN 2)
f
Fade out
Alt. Res Pattern (see notes)

11
(x3 - 5)
Fade in
11a
TAPE TRK 2 (VIOLIN 1)
APE TRK 2 (VIOLIN 3)
Result of TAPE TRK. 2 (VIOLINS 1-3)
(x3 - 5)
VIOLIN (VIOLIN 2)
f
alt. Res. Pattern (see notes)
11b
(x3 - 6)
Fade out

12
13
TAPE TRK. 2 (VIOLIN 1)
hold tempo 1
hold tempo 1
TAPE TRK. 2 (VIOLIN 3)
hold tempo 1
hold tempo 1
(x8-12)
(x6-16)
(x8-16)
(x6-16)
VIOLIN (VIOLIN 2)
accel. v. slightly
hold tempo 1
accel. v. slightly
Fade in
mf
14
15
hold tempo 1
hold tempo 1
hold tempo 1
hold tempo 1
(x8-16)
(x6-16)
(x8-16)
(x6-16)
hold tempo 1
accel. v. slightly
hold tempo 1
accel. v. slightly
16
17
TAPE TRACK 2 (VIOLIN 1)
TAPE TRACK 2 (VIOLIN 3)
(x4-8)
TAPE TRACK 1 (VIOLIN 4)
Fade in
mf
(x4-8)
(x4-8)
VIOLIN (VIOLIN 2)
hold tempo 1
Fade out
18
19
TAPE TRK. 2 (VIOLIN 1)
hold tempo 1
TAPE TRK. 2 (VIOLIN 3)
hold tempo 1
TAPE TRK. 1 (VIOLIN 4)
hold tempo 1
Result of TAPE TRKS. 1+2 (VIOLINS 1+3+4)
tempo 1
(x4-8)
(x2-4)
(x2-6)
(V)
(V)
VIOLIN (VIOLIN 2)
accel. v. slightly
Fade in
f
All Res Pattern (see notes)
accel. v. slightly

19a
19b
hold tempo 1
tempo 1
(x3-6)
(x2-6)
accel. v. slightly
accel v slightly
19c
19d
(x2-6)
Fade out
20
20a
TAPE TRK 2 (VIOLIN 1)
TAPE TRK 2 (VIOLIN 3)
TAPE TRK 1 (VIOLIN 4)
Result of TAPE TRKS 1 + 2 (VIOLINS 1+3+4)
VIOLIN (VIOLIN 2)
Fade in
All Res Pattern (see notes)
(x2-4)

20b
20c
hold tempo 1
tempo 1
(x2-4)
accel v slightly
accel. v. slightly
20d
21
TAPE TRK. 2
(VIOLIN 1)
TAPE TRK 2
(VIOLIN 3)
TAPE TRK. 1
(VIOLIN 4)
Result of
TAPE TRKS. 1 + 2
(VIOLINS 1+3+4)
(x3-6)
(x2-6)
VIOLIN
(VIOLIN 2)
Fade out
Fade in
f
Alt. Res.
Pattern
(see notes)
21a
21b
TAPE TRACK 2
(VIOLIN 1)
TAPE TRACK 2
(VIOLIN 3)
TAPE TRACK 1
(VIOLIN 4)
Result of
TAPE TRKS. 1 + 2
(VIOLINS 1+3+4)
VIOLIN
(VIOLIN 2)
Alt Res.
Pattern
(see notes)

21c
21d
hold tempo 1
hold tempo 1
hold tempo 1
tempo 1
(x3-6)
(x2-6)
(x3-6)
hold tempo 1
accel. v slightly
hold tempo 1
Fade out
hold tempo 1
accel v slightly
hold tempo 1
22
22a
TAPE TRK. 2 (VIOLIN 1)
TAPE TRK. 2 (VIOLIN 3)
TAPE TRK. 1 (VIOLIN 4)
Result of TAPE TRKS 1+2 (VIOLINS 1+3+4)
(x3-5)
VIOLIN (VIOLIN 2)
Fade in
All. Res. Pattern (see notes)
22b
22c
(x3-5)
f

22d
22e
APE TRK. 2 (VIOLIN 1)
PE TRK. 2 (VIOLIN 3)
PE TRK. 1 (VIOLIN 4)
Result of APE TRKS. 1+2 VIOLINS 1+3+4
(x3-5)
VIOLIN (VIOLIN 2)
fade out
Alt. Res. Pattern (see notes)
22f
22g
23
23a
APE TRK. 2 (VIOLIN 1)
APE TRK. 2 (VIOLIN 3)
APE TRK. 1 (VIOLIN 4)
Result of APE TRKS. 1+2 (VIOLINS 1+3+4)
(x3-5)
(x6-8)
CUE for End (see notes)
VIOLIN (VIOLIN 2)
Fade in
f
Oct. 1967

37. Louis Andriessen (b. 1939)
De Staat, mm. 1-161 (1972-76)

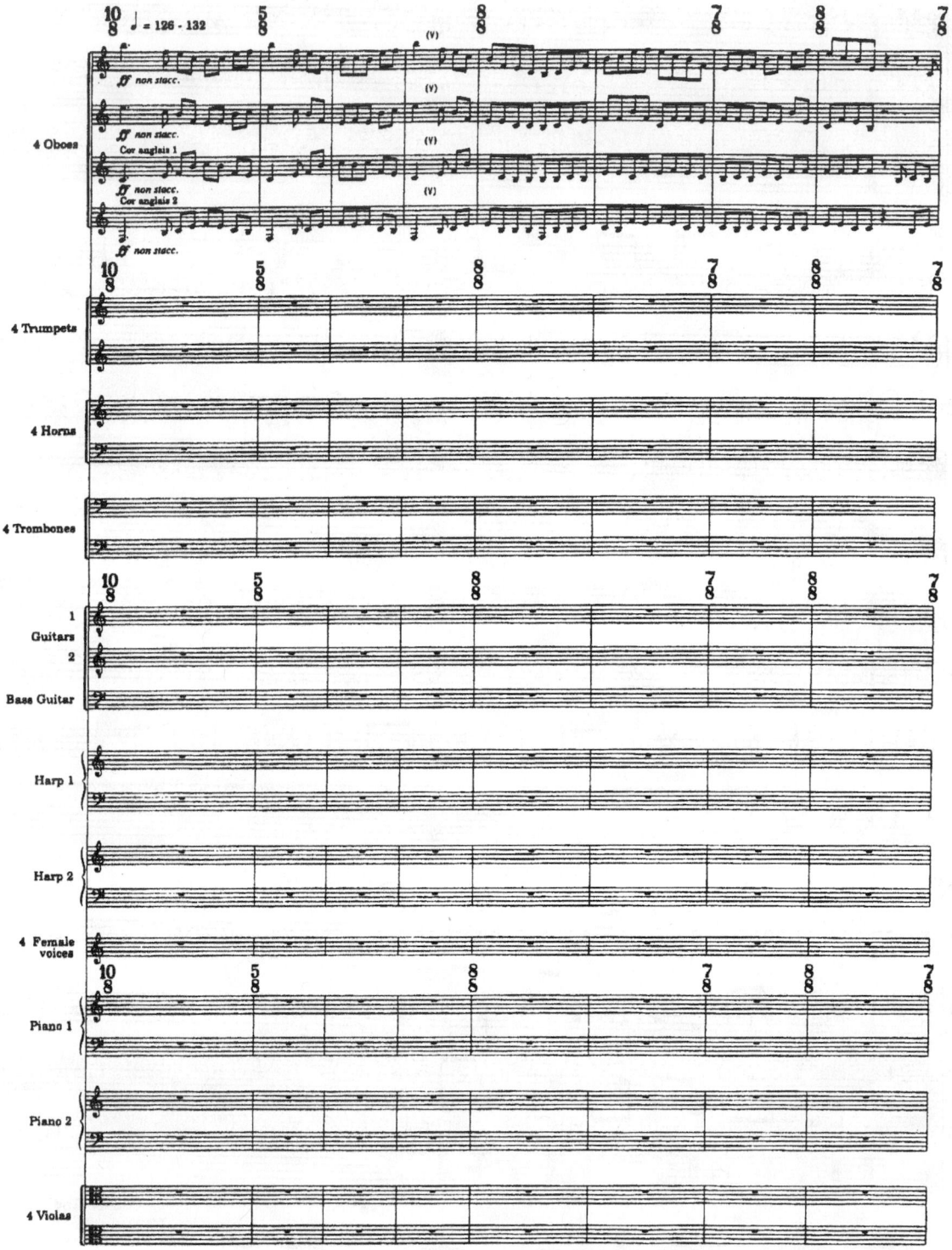

N.B.: All instruments in this score are notated in C.

9
Ob. 1
Ob. 2
C.A. 1
C.A. 2
17
25
non dim.
f
1
35
simile
ff
2

45
Ob. 1
Ob. 2
C.A. 1
C.A. 2
55
Ob. 1
Ob. 2
C.A. 1
C.A. 2
63
Ob. 1
Ob. 2
C.A. 1
C.A. 2
change to oboe
change to oboe
Tbne 1
Tbne 2
Tbne 3
Tbne 4
simile
ff non stacc.
sempre marcatissimo

71
Tbne 1
Tbne 2
Tbne 3
Tbne 4
81
Hn. 1
Hn. 2
Hn. 3
Hn. 4
4 molto forte e pesante
ff pesante non stacc.
marc. pesante
cresc.
sff
ff pesante
88

97
Ob. 1.2
Ob. 3.4
Hn. 1
Hn. 2
Hn. 3
Hn. 4
sempre crescendo
Tbne 1
Tbne 2
Tbne 3
Tbne 4
Guit. 1
Guit. 2
B. Git.
Harp 1
Harp 2
Fem. v.
Pno 1
Pno 2
Vla 1.2
Vla 3.4

*) open strings

112
Ob. 1.2
Ob. 3.4
Tr. 1.2
Tr. 3.4
Hn. 1.2
Hn. 3.4
Tbne 1.2
Tbne 3.4
Guit. 1
Guit. 2
B.Guit.
Harp 1
Harp 2
Fem. v.
ni - ān kai rhüth - mon tē lek - sei, o - li - gū pros tēn au -
Pno 1
Pno 2
Vla 1.2
Vla 3.4
a2

121
Ob. 1.2
Ob. 3.4
Tr. 1.2
Tr. 3.4
Hn. 1.2
Hn. 3.4
Tbne 1.2
Tbne 3.4
Guit. 1
Guit. 2
B.Guit.
Harp 1
Harp 2
Fem. v.
div. a 2
a4
tēn ging - ne - tai
le - gein tō or - thōs le - gon - ti kai en
Pno 1
Pno 2
Vla 1.2
Vla 3.4

130
6
Ob. 1.2
Ob. 3.4
Tr. 1.2
Tr. 3.4
Hn. 1.2
Hn. 3.4
Tbne 1.2
Tbne 3.4
6
Guit. 1
Guit. 2
B.Guit.
Harp 1
Harp 2
Fem. v.
miä har - mo - ni - ä
smik - rai
gar hai me - ta - bo -
6
Pno 1
Pno 2
Vla 1.2
gliss.
Vla 3.4

139
Ob. 1.2
Ob. 3.4
Tr. 1.2
Tr. 3.4
Hn. 1.2
Hn. 3.4
Tbne 1.2
Tbne 3.4
Guit. 1
Guit. 2
B.Guit.
Harp 1
Harp 2
Fem. v.
lai kai dē en rhüth - mō hō - sau - tōs pa - ra - plē - si - ō
Pno 1
Pno 2
Vla 1.2
Vla 3.4

148
7
Ob. 1.2
Ob. 3.4
cresc.
Tr. 1.2
Tr. 3.4
Hn. 1.2
Hn. 3.4
Tbne 1.2
Tbne 3.4
Guit. 1
Guit. 2
B.Guit.
Harp 1
Harp 2
Fem. v.
(grace note on the beat)
ti - ni?
ko-mi-dē men ūn,
e - phē,
hū - tōs e - khei.
a4
Pno 1
Pno 2
Vla 1.2
Vla 3.4
non div.
div.

157
Ob. 1.2
Ob. 3.4
Tr. 1.2
Tr. 3.4
Hn. 1.2
Hn. 3.4
Tbne 1.2
Tbne 3.4
Guit. 1
Guit. 2
B.Guit.
Harp 1
l.v.
Harp 2
l.v.
Fem. v.
non dim.
Pno 1
stacc.
ff
senza Ped.
Pno 2
fff
Vla 1.2
Vla 3.4
*) no accent on low g

38. Arvo Pärt (b. 1935)
Cantus (1977)

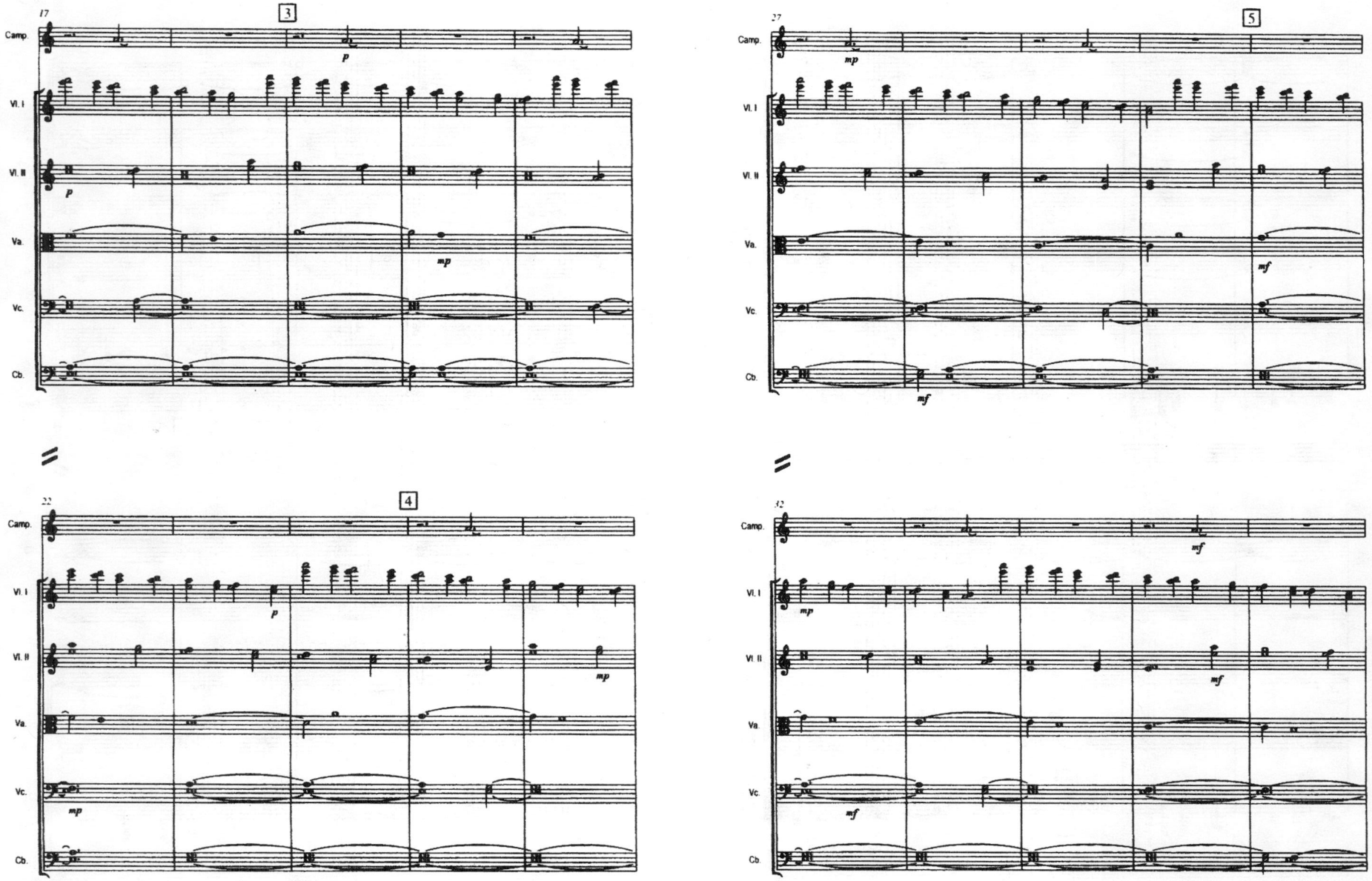
17
3
Camp.
p
Vl. I
Vl. II
p
Va.
mp
Vc.
Cb.
22
4
Camp.
Vl. I
p
Vl. II
mp
Va.
Vc.
mp
Cb.
27
5
Camp.
mp
Vl. I
Vl. II
Va.
mf
Vc.
Cb.
mf
32
Camp.
mf
Vl. I
mp
Vl. II
mf
Va.
Vc.
mf
Cb.

6
Camp.
Vl. I
Vl. II
Va.
Vc.
Cb.
mf
f

7
Camp.
Vl. I
Vl. II
Va.
Vc
Cb.
f

8
Camp.
Vl. I
Vl. II
Va.
Vc.
Cb.
f

9
Camp
Vl. I
Vl. II
Va.
Vc.
div.
Cb.
div. *)
ff
p
*) 2 soli (1° leggio)

57
10
Camp.
fff
div.
uniti
Vl. I
Vl. II
Va.
Vc.
div.
Cb.
62
uniti
rIV
fff
67
11
12
ff
div.
uniti
74
13
f
uniti
rIV

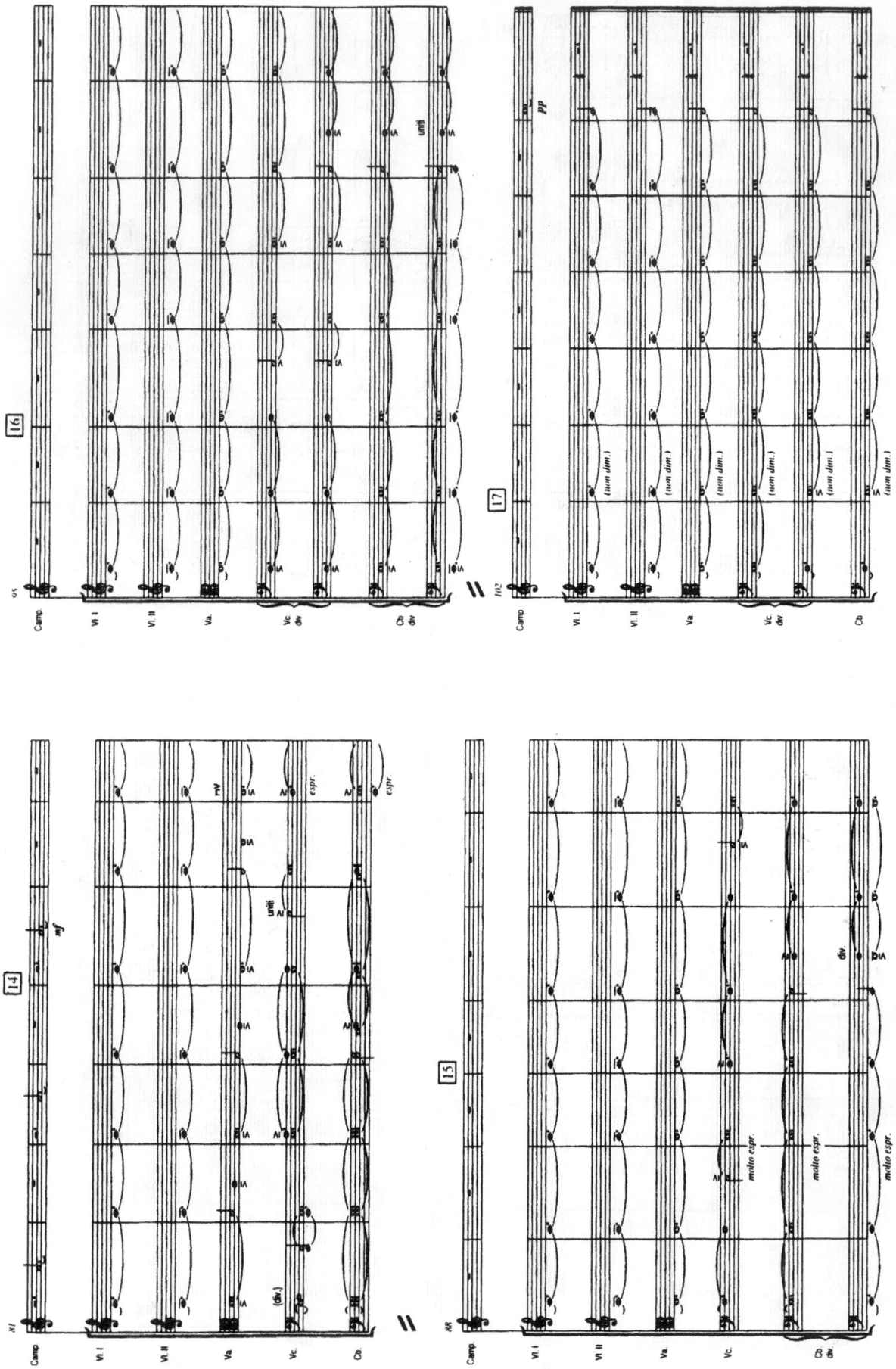
14
15
16
17
Camp.
Vl. I
Vl. II
Va.
Vc.
Cb.
mf
mV
espr.
unis
(div.)
molto espr.
div.
pp
(non div.)

39. Augusta Read Thomas (b. 1964)

Spring Song, mm. 1-41 (1995)

*Play measures 16-33 as one long phrase, with subphrases of measures 16-24, 25-27, 28-30, 31, and 32.

22
accel.
3:2
ff sempre
25
♩= 80
3:2
rit.
a tempo (♩= 80)
28
III
IV
severe
II
III
3:2
Molto intenso, bell-like (♩= 104-112)
32
(ff sempre)
35
37
3:2
rit.
41

40. Thomas Adès (b. 1971)

Asyla, II, mm. 1-43 (1997)

N.B.: All instruments in this score are notated in C.

A
B
Fl.
B. Cl.
solo
mf molto cantabile, espr.
Cl.
1–3, soli
ppp spettrale ma cantab.
Bsn.
Chsn.
Hn.
Tpt.
1–3 practice mutes, quite hard-blown
(sound) pp molto espr.
Tbn.
Tba.
Perc. 2
(Cowbells)
Pno. 1
r.h. legatissimo
(inside flutes)
Upright
Pno. 2
Celesta
(hold on Upright IV)
r.h.: Celesta
r.h.: Upright
r.h.: Celesta
off)
ppp sempre (inside clarinets)
Cel: con molto
Hp.
f sub.
p
l.v.
A
B
Vln. I
senza vib.
unis. arco
sul tasto
ppp poss., legatissimo poss.
Vln. II
unis. arco sul tasto
senza vib.
ppp poss., legatissimo poss.
Vla. div.
(pizz.) alla chitarra
ppp accompagnando
Vc.
Db.

C
Fl.
B. Cl.
più piangendo
poco f
(a3)
Cl.
3. to Contrabass Clarinet
ppp sempre
(con sord. if poss.)
ppp poss.
Bsn.
play only if Bsn 1 plays con sord.
con sord.
ppp poss.
Cbsn.
ppp
1. solo, con sord.
forced tone, cantab.
via sord.
3. (senza sord.)
mp quasi f, molto piangendo
pp piangendo
Hn.
2. solo, con sord. forced tone, cantab.
via sord.
mp quasi f, molto piangendo
4. (senza sord.)
pp piangendo
(a3)
Tpt.
3. to Piccolo Trumpet
a2 practice mutes
Tbn.
via sord.
(sound) ppp sempre
poco
solo molto cantab.
Tba.
ppp
mp
Perc.
Pno. I
mf (sub.)
ppp
pp
poco f
raise
off
Cel.
pp
release Practise Pedal on Upright
Hp.
mp
p
portamento (legatissimo)
C
Vln. I
Vln. II
Vla.
Vc.
Db.
1. solo pizz.
desk 1
div. pizz.
ppp
* these two breaths if absolutely necessary (b. 27 & 31)

D
slargando al
Fl.
Ob.
B. Ob.
Cl.
Cb. Cl.
Bsn.
Cbsn.
Hn.
Tpt.
Picc. Tpt.
Tbn.
Tba
Cowbells
Perc. 3
Pno. 1
Hp.
(to Cor Anglais ad lib.)
straight mutes - gradually remove
senza sord (slightly covered)
solo, straight mute
1-3 senza sord
B.D. senza sord
(to Grand)
Vln. I
third last desk
last 2 desks
Vln. II
div.
6 soli 2,3
Vla
4-6
Vc.
2 soli
Db
(sul tasto)
pizz.
arco
tutti div. a2
sul ponti.
ord. (non trem.)
sul tasto
arco sul ponti.
desk 1 arco
last desk arco
tutti arco div. a2
unis.
ord.

rit.
a tempo
Fl.
Ob.
B. Ob.
Cl.
Cb. Cl.
Bsn.
Cbsn.
Hn.
Tpt.
Pic. Tpt.
Tbn.
B. Tbn.
Tba.
Perc. 3
Pno. I (Grand)
Hp.
Vln. I
Vln. II
Vla.
Vc.
Db.
2. to Cor Anglais
(ossia: Cor Anglais)
con sord. subito
2. solo (straight mute)
2. take straight mute subito
to Trumpet in B♭
straight mutes subito possibile
(Cowbells)
(B.D.)
sempre
niente
tutti
div.
unis.
non trem.
sul tasto
ord.
poco sul pont.
molto espr.
mp sub.

40
E
♩ = 50-54
Fl.
solo senza vib.
B. Cl.
molto
to Clarinet in A
Cl.
Cb. Cl.
Bsn.
Chan.
Hn.
1,3 con sord.
2,4 con sord.
Tpt.
Tbn.
Perc. 2
(Cowbells)
soft beaters (at least 2 players)
dolciss. sempre
Pno. 1
place thick folded cloth over the strings
and weigh down firmly enough to damp most of the resona
Hp.
Vln. I
practice mute
arco
Vln. II
div.
3 soli from last two desks (div. a3)
practice mutes
Vla.
div.
Vc.
div.
pizz.
ord.
Db
div.
sul tasto

41. Kaija Saariaho (b. 1952)

Ariel's Hail (2000)

11
mp poco dolce
thy best plea-sure;
be it to fly,
mp
mp
pp
mp
f
ord.
mp
14
mf più energico
poco agitato
To swim,
to dive in - to fire,
mp
mp
mp
f
p
mp
17
f agitato
Calando
to ride On the curled clouds;
mf agitato
f
f
mp

20
Calmo
mp
to thy strong bid-ding
mp
f
mp
sfz
23
mf
rallentando....
task
A - ri - el, and all his qua - li - ty.
mp
26
A tempo
mf calmo
I boar-ded the King's
molto vibr.
mp sfz
mp
f
mf
mp poco sfz
mp sfz
mf

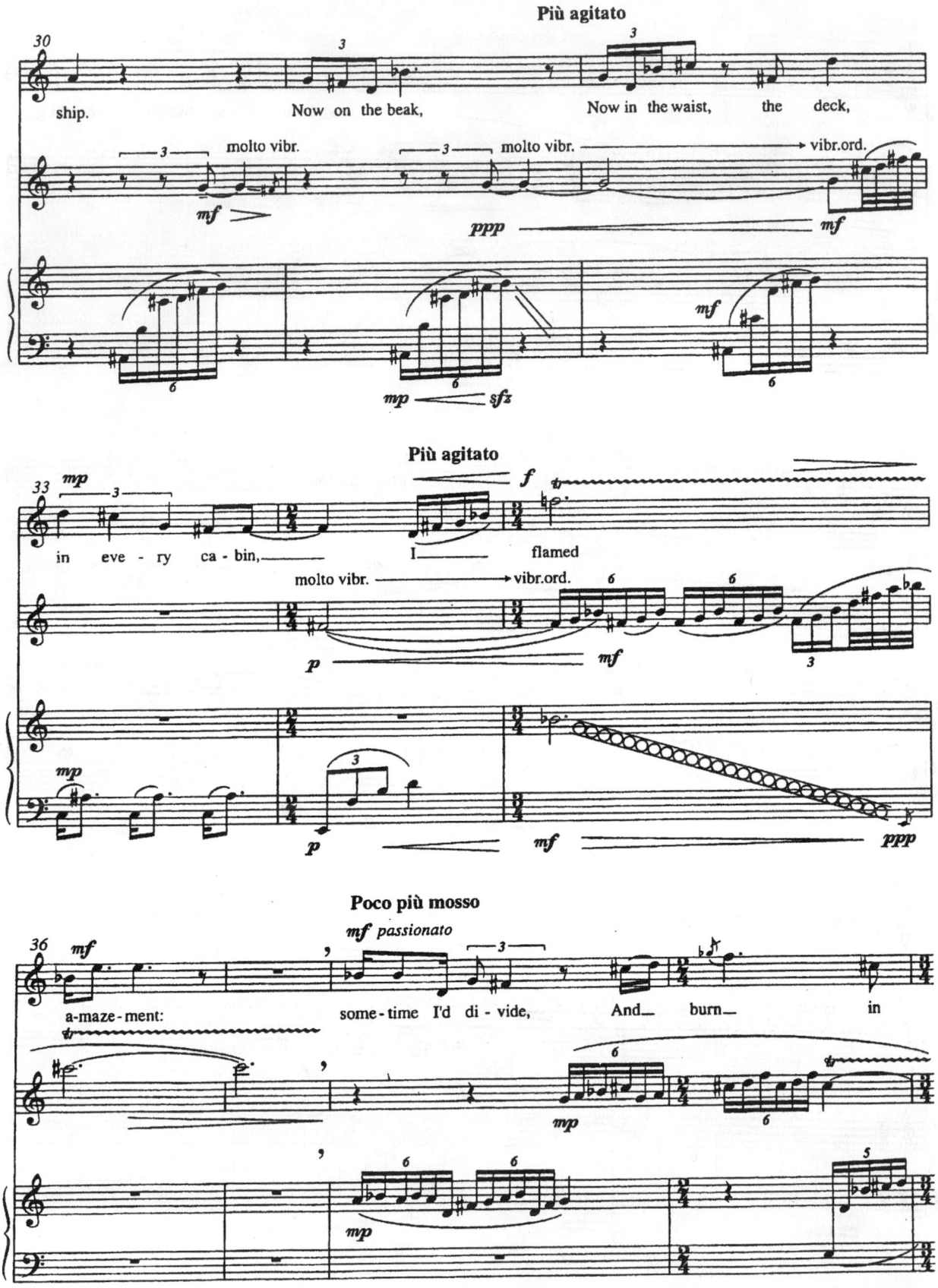
Più agitato
30
ship.
Now on the beak,
Now in the waist,
the deck,
molto vibr.
molto vibr.
vibr.ord.
mf
ppp
mf
mf
mp
sfz
Più agitato
33
mp
f
in eve - ry ca - bin,
I
flamed
molto vibr.
vibr.ord.
p
mf
mp
p
mf
ppp
Poco più mosso
36
mf
mf passionato
a-maze-ment:
some-time I'd di - vide,
And
burn
in
mp
mp

A tempo primo
rallentando....
mp calmo ma giocoso
40
ma - ny pla - ces.
Then I beat my ta - bor, At
calando
mp
43
which, like un - backed colts, they pricked their ears,
molto vibr.
mp
mp
mp
mp
47
Ad - vanced their eye - lids, lif - ted up their no - ses As they
vibr ord.
mp
mp
près de la table

51
mp
dolce, espressivo
smelt
mu - sic,
S.V.
so I
molto vibr.
p
mf
ord.
p
mp
55
rallentando....
Meno mosso
p
charmed their ears,
I charmed their
molto vibr.
vibr.ord.
mp
p
60
ears.
pp
mf
mp
mf
mp
pp
Paris, 17 Sept. 2000

Acknowledgment of Sources

1. Debussy PRELUDES, BOOK 1 © 1985 by Wiener Urtext Edition, Musikverlag Ges. M.b.H & Co. K.G., Wien. All rights reserved. Used by permission of European American Music Distributors LLC, U.S. and Canadian agent for Wiener Urtext Edition, Musikverelag Ges. M.b.H & Co. K.G., Wien.
2. Debussy CANOPE Copyright by Dover Publications, Inc. All rights reserved under Pan American and International Copyright Conventions.
3. SARABANDE from POUR LE PIANO By Claude Debussy. Edited by Gaby Casadesus. Copyright © 1986, 1987 by G. Schirmer, Inc. (ASCAP) International Copyright Secured. All Rights Reserved. Reprinted by permission.
4. Stravinsky RITE OF SPRING Copyright by Dover Publications, Inc. All rights reserved under Pan American and International Copyright Conventions.
5. SONG OF THE HARVEST from 44 DUOS (Bartók) © Copyright 1933 in t he USA by Boosey & Hawkes, Inc. Copyright renewed. Reprinted by permission.
6. WHOLE-TONE SCALE, MIKROKOSMOS (Bartók) © Copyright 1940 by Boosey & Hawkes Music Publishers Ltd. Copyright Renewed. Reprinted by permission of Boosey & Hawkes, Inc.
7. DIMINISHED FIFTH, MIKROKOSMOS © Copyright 1940 by Hawkes & Son (London) Ltd. Copyright Renewed. Definitive corrected edition © Copyright 1987 by Hawkes & Son (London) Ltd. Reprinted by permission of Boosey & Hawkes, Inc.
8. FROM THE ISLAND OF BALI, MIKROKOSMOS (Béla Bartók) © Copyright 1940 by Hawkes & Son (London) Ltd. Copyright Renewed. Definitive corrected edition © Copyright 1987 by Hawkes & Son (London) Ltd. Reprinted by permission of Boosey & Hawkes, Inc.
9. Webern FIVE MOVEMENTS FOR STRING QUARTET, OP. 5 © 1922 by Universal Edition © renewed. Used by permission of European American Music Distributors LLC, U.S. and Canadian agent for Universal Corporation, sole U.S. agent for Universal Edition (London) Ltd., London.
10. Webern FIVE MOVEMENTS FOR STRING QUARTET, OP. 5 © 1922 by Universal Edition © renewed. Used by permission of European American Music Distributors LLC, U.S. and Canadian agent for Universal Corporation, sole U.S. agent for Universal Edition (London) Ltd., London.
11. Schoenberg BOOK OF THE HANGING GARDENS Copyright © renewed 1941 by Arnold Schoenberg. Used by permission of Belmont Music Publishers.
12. Berg FOUR SONGS, OP. 2 © 1928 by Robert Lienau Musikverlag, Frankfurt am Main (Germany). Copyright Renewed. Reprinted by permission.
13. AGNUS DEI from MASS (Stravinsky) © Copyright 1948 by Hawkes & Son (London) Ltd. Copyright renewed. Reprinted by permission of Boosey & Hawkes, Inc.
14. Hindemith LUDUS TONALIS © Schott & Co. Ltd., London 1943. © renewed 1971. All Rights Reserved. Used by permission of European American Music Distributors LLC, sole U.S. and Canadian agent for Schott & Co. Ltd., London.
15. Hindemith DAS MARIENLEBEN © 1924 by Schott Musik International © renewed. All Rights Reserved. Used by permission of European American Music Distributors LLC, sole U.S. and Canadian agent for Schott Musik International.
16. Ives 114 SONGS Copright © 1955 by Peer International Corporation. International copyright secured. Printed in U.S.A. All rights reserved including the right of public performance for profit. Copyright renewed 1984.
17. Ives 114 SONGS Copright © 1955 by Peer International Corporation. International copyright secured. Printed in U.S.A. All rights reserved including the right of public performance for profit. Copyright renewed 1984.
18. Crawford Seeger DIAPHONIC SUITE NO. 4 © 1972 by Continuo Music Press, Inc. Sole Agent: Masters Music, a division of Kalmus, Inc. Reprinted with permission.
19. Dallapiccola QUADERNO MUSICALE DI ANNALIBERA No. 5 "Contrapunctus secundus." Reprinted by permission of SugarMusic Spa.
20. Dallapiccola QUADERNO MUSICALE DI ANNALIBERA No. 11 "Quartina." Reprinted by permission of SugarMusic Spa.
21. Webern THREE SONGS, OP. 25 © 1956 by Universal Edition A.G. Wien © renewed. Used by permission of European American Music Distributors LLC, U.S. and Canadian agent for Universal Edition A.G., Wien.
22. Webern PIANO VARIATIONS, OP. 27 © 1937 by Universal Edition © renewed. Used by permission of European American Music Distributors LLC, U.S. and Canadian agent for Universal Edition.

23. Schoenberg KLAVIERSTÜCK OP. 33a © 1929 by Universal Edition. © renewed 1956. Used by permission of Belmont Music Publishers.
24. REQUIEM CANTICLES (Stravinsky) © Copyright 1967 by Boosey & Hawkes Music Publishers Ltd. Copyright Renewed. Reprinted by permission of Boosey & Hawkes, Inc.
25. Boulez STRUCTURES © 1955 by Universal Edition (London) Ltd., London © renewed. All Rights Reserved. Used by permission of European American Music Distributors LLC, U.S. and Canadian agent for Universal Edition (London) Ltd., London.
26. COMPOSITION FOR 12 INSTRUMENTS By Milton Babbitt Copyright © 1964 (Renewed) by Associated Music Publishers, Inc., (BMI) International Copyright Secured. All Rights Reserved. Reprinted by Permission.
27. Messiaen TURANGALILA SYMPHONY © 1953 by Durand & Cie.
28. STRING QUARTET NO. 1 By Elliott Carter. Copyright © 1961 (Renewed) by Associated Music Publishers, Inc. (BMI) International Copyright Secured. All Rights Reserved. Reprinted by Permission.
29. Stokhausen STIMMUNG © 1981 by Universal Edition A.G., Wien. All Rights Reserved. Used by permission of European American Music Distributors LLC, U.S. and Canadian agent for Universal Edition A.G., Wien.
30. Cage WINTER MUSIC © 1960 by Henmar Press, Inc., sole selling agent C.F. Peters Corporation. All rights reserved. Used by permission.
31. Lutosławski JEUX VENITIENS © 1962 by Moeck Verlag & Musikinstrumente, Celle, Germany © renewed. All Rights Reserved. Used by permission of European American Music Distributors LLC, sole U.S. and Canadian agent for Moeck Verlag & Musikinstrumente, Celle, Germany.
32. Ligeti RAMIFICATIONS © 1970 by Schott Musik International © renewed. All Rights Reserved. Used by permission of European American Music Distributors LLC, sole U.S. and Canadian agent for Schott Musik International.
33. *Music for the Magic Theater,* Reh. 1-17 by Rochberg © 1972 Theodore Presser Co, Bryn Mawr, PA
34. Berio SINFONIA © 1969 by Universal Edition (London) Ltd., London © renewed. All Rights Reserved. Used by permission of European American Music Distributors LLC, U.S. and Canadian agent for Universal Edition (London) Ltd., London.
35. Crumb MAKROKOSMOS Vol. 1 no. 11 © 1974 by C. F. Peters Corp., NY. Reprinted with permission.
36. Reich VIOLIN PHASE © 1969 by Universal Edition (London) Ltd. London © renewed. Used by permission of European American Music Distributors LLC, U.S. and Canadian agent for Universal Corporation, sole U.S. agent for Universal Edition (London) Ltd., London.
37. DE STAAT (Andriessen) © Copyright 1994 by Boosey & Hawkes Music Publishers, Ltd. Reprinted by permission of Boosey & Hawkes, Inc.
38. Pärt CANTUS IN MEMORY OF BENJAMIN BRITTEN © 1981 by Universal Edition A.G., Wien. All Rights Reserved. Used by permission of European American Music Distributors LLC, U.S. and Canadian agent for Universal Edition A.G., Wien.
39. SPRING SONG By Augusta Read Thomas Copyright © 1995 by G. Schirmer, Inc. (ASCAP) International copyright secured. All Rights Reserved. Reprinted by permission.
40. Adès ASYLA © 1997 by Faber Music. Reprinted by kind permission of the publishers.
41. ARIEL'S HAIL From THE TEMPEST SONGBOOK Music by Kaija Saariaho, Words by William Shakespeare. Copyright © 2000 Chester Music Limited, London, United Kingdom. International Copyright Secured. All Rights Reserved.